Listener's Handbook

A Guide to Music Appreciation

Listener's Handbook

A Guide to Music Appreciation

IRA SCHROEDER

Associate Professor, Department of Music
Iowa State University

THE IOWA STATE UNIVERSITY PRESS, AMES
1966

IRA SCHROEDER, associate professor of music at Iowa State University, is a world-renowned carillonneur. He has taught classes in music appreciation since 1949, as well as teaching piano. He has been President of the Guild of Carillonneurs in North America and was responsible for editing and publishing carillon music for the Guild. He has traveled extensively throughout the United States, Canada, and Europe appearing as guest carillonneur as well as being university carillonneur at Iowa State. The author received his B.Mus. degree from Bush Conservatory of Music, Chicago, in 1927. He came to Iowa State University in 1931 after teaching for four years at Bush.

First edition, 1958

Second edition, 1962
Second printing, 1963
Third printing, 1964

Third edition, 1966
Second printing, 1967

Library of Congress Catalog Card Number: 66–14367

PREFACE

THIS BOOK is written for listeners who know little or nothing about the various kinds of music literature and for those who are already acquainted with a great deal of music and wish to explore further. Anyone can learn to understand and enjoy listening to music if he wants to. We all have the ability and can develop the capacity to appreciate the best in music even though we may not know one note from another or have any knowledge about the technical side of either composing or performing. The listener is the third party. Listening to and understanding music takes time and effort but the reward is well worthwhile.

At no time in history has there been so great an opportunity to hear the best of music performed by the finest artists. This is made possible through radio, television, and recordings, the last of which is the most important. Since we all tend to enjoy most the music we are best acquainted with, what better way can we find to become familiar with music than by having a record to hear over and over when we want to?

Then there comes a time when we have heard our favorite piece enough and we want to branch out into new fields. Because of the literally endless variety in music, these exploratory journeys can become extremely interesting and fascinating.

This book, organized to assist the beginner, will help him find his way around in the various periods and trends of musical development, will help him find the different kinds of music that may interest him, help him organize and set up his own library of recorded music and, best of all, show him avenues of exploration.

The technical terms are explained in ordinary language and the reader is given insight as to how to listen to various kinds of music and what to expect of the music itself. There is music to reflect every mood and occasion.

In the space arts we often find examples of paintings, buildings or sculpturing that are considered mediocre or poor artistically. For economic reasons, many buildings of poor design survive for many years, even centuries, but in music we do not need to be concerned about what is good or bad because only worthwhile music has survived. In this the beginner must trust. According to estimates, about 90 per cent of all music written as serious music fails to stand the test of time.

The suggestions listed in each category are among the more interesting or appealing in that particular classification.

So often we hear someone say, "I know what I like." What he is really saying is that he likes what he knows. If you are a cooperative, receptive, attentive listener, you will have endless hours of pleasure in exploring the field of music. Listening to music is a very satisfying hobby that can be shared with many. It is one of the arts that makes up the most important art of all —the art of living.

IRA SCHROEDER

CONTENTS

Listener's Handbook

A Guide to Music Appreciation

Chapter One

THE ELEMENTS OF MUSIC

MUSIC has seven elements. They are: (1) rhythm, (2) melody, (3) harmony, (4) tempo, (5) dynamics, (6) form, and (7) color. Sometimes one or more of these elements are more important or predominant than others.

(1) Rhythm, for all practical purposes, is regular recurring accents. It is sometimes referred to as "meter." Except in irregular rhythms, often found in twentieth-century music, accents divide the beats into groups of twos or threes, or multiples of these. For example, the waltz has an accent on the first beat of each group of three beats—ONE, two, three—ONE, two, three—etc. A march usually has a strong accent on the first beat of each group of four and a lesser accent on the third beat—*ONE*, two, *Three*, four—*ONE*, two, *Three*, four—etc.

(2) A melody may be very simply defined as a "tune." It may be very evident or a little obscure. Melodies or melodic lines may or may not be singable. So often someone complains about music—especially some twentieth-century music—saying, "It has no tune." Melodies of different periods, different trends and different composers vary in type and degree of importance. All music has melody, but sometimes the rhythm or some other element is more important.

(3) Harmony is the chordal structure or a combination of tones that are sounded simultaneously. These combinations may sound happy, sad, plaintive or any number of describable or in-

describable ways. There are those chords or combinations of tones that are dissonant. These serve a definite purpose. They create vigor and give the music added character and contrast.

Paintings are not all sweet, depicting the beautiful. Think of the number of masterpieces of the Crucifixion—the saints being burned at the stake! Sweet lullaby music would certainly be out of place as a counterpart to these.

(4) Tempo is the speed at which a composition is taken. A funeral march has an entirely different effect than a military march. Tempo is an element of expression in all of the time arts such as music, drama, ballet, movies, radio, and television. In a drama, tempo is very important because different moods require different speeds. For example, it would be just as ridiculous to have slow conversation about an exciting football game as it would be to have fast conversation at the bedside of a dying friend. In music, tempo is just as important in portraying various moods.

(5) Dynamics in music means volume. This is an element of expression relating directly to the mood or drama of the music. A ballet of sylphs might be accompanied very softly by a harp but a rough and ready gypsy dance would require a much louder and more rugged type of music.

(6) Form is the design or the structure of music. All music has some sort of structure varying from a strict form to a very free form. By strict form we mean music that conforms to definite patterns such as rondo, ternary form, and sonata form (see Glossary). By free form we mean a composition that is developed with unity and a feeling of balance without holding to patterns. Strict and free form may be likened to formal and informal gardens. The formal garden has definite design while the informal has a more "natural" appearance, yet the informal has a "feeling" of organization.

(7) Color in music is the psychological interpretation of the quality of sound produced by any instrument(s), voice(s), device(s), or any combination thereof. We think of bright or dark colors in connection with the timbre or tone color of the different orchestral instruments, combinations of instruments, human voices, and the changes of the human voice that occur under different emotional circumstances. The top range of the brilliant trumpet, for example, is much brighter in color than the low tones of the tuba.

4

Chapter Two

INSTRUMENTS OF THE
SYMPHONY ORCHESTRA

THE INSTRUMENTS of the orchestra are divided into four choirs. They are the string, woodwind, brass, and percussion choirs. Symphony orchestras differ greatly in seating plans and number of individual instruments. The following is an outline of the instruments in their various choirs.

ORGANIZATION AND SEATING PLAN OF THE CONVENTIONAL SYMPHONY ORCHESTRA

I. Stringed Instruments (String Choir)
   Violins
   Violas
   Violoncellos (Cellos)
   Double-basses
   Harp
   Harpsichord
   Piano (sometimes classified as percussion)
II. Woodwind Instruments (Woodwind Choir)
   Piccolo (no reed)
   Flutes (no reed)
   Clarinets (one reed)
   Saxophones (one reed)
   Oboes (two reeds)
   English Horns (two reeds)
   Bassoons (two reeds)
   Contrabassoons (two reeds)

III. Brass Instruments (Brass Choir)
   Trumpets
   Cornets (seldom used any more)
   French Horns
   Trombones
   Tubas
IV. Percussion Instruments (Percussion Choir)

Timpani (Kettledrums)	Glockenspiel
Bass Drum	Xylophone
Side Drum	Castanets
Snare Drum	Tambourine
Chimes	Celesta
Cymbals	Marimba
Gong	Vibraphone
Triangle	Etc., etc.,

DESCRIPTION OF THE INSTRUMENTS

Within the choirs are families of instruments. For example, the violin family is made up of the violin, viola, violoncello, and double bass. These may be called soprano, alto, tenor, and bass. Members of the same family of instruments not only produce their musical sounds in the same way but have somewhat the same timbre. Timbre is the quality of color of the sound of an individual instrument or human voice. For example, various instruments and voices, when sounding the same pitch, have different tone qualities. This must not be confused wth orchestral tone color. Orchestral tone color is produced by a combination of orchestral instruments. It is usually thought of in connection with a combination of instruments of different timbre.

The harp, harpsichord, and piano are not of the same family, as is sometimes thought. These instruments have different ancestors and each produces its sound in a different way. The strings of the harp are plucked by the fingers. The harpsichord is a keyboard instrument quite similar to the piano in appearance but the timbre is quite different because the strings are sounded by a plucking mechanism instead of a hammer action like that of the piano. The timbre is somewhat like that of a mandolin or a guitar. Harpsichords vary in size from very small to very large. The smaller ones look somewhat like tiny spinet pianos or tiny grand pianos. The larger ones look like large grand pianos. Harpsichords may have one or two keyboards. The keyboards of the two-keyboard harpsichords are placed similarly to the keyboards of a two-manual pipe organ.

6

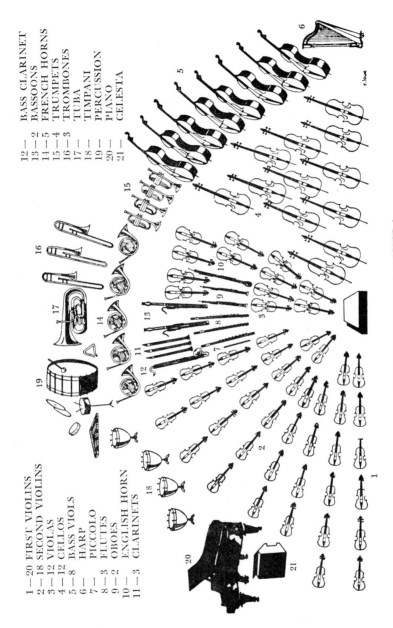

1 — 20 FIRST VIOLINS
2 — 18 SECOND VIOLINS
3 — 12 VIOLAS
4 — 12 CELLOS
5 — 8 BASS VIOLS
6 — HARP
7 — PICCOLO
8 — 3 FLUTES
9 — 2 OBOES
10 — ENGLISH HORN
11 — 3 CLARINETS

12 — BASS CLARINET
13 — 2 BASSOONS
14 — 5 FRENCH HORNS
15 — 4 TRUMPETS
16 — 3 TROMBONES
17 — TUBA
18 — TIMPANI
19 — PERCUSSION
20 — PIANO
21 — CELESTA

r. lowe

SYMPHONY ORCHESTRA

A SEATING PLAN

7

RANGES OF MUSICAL INSTRUMENTS

IN RELATION TO THE PIANO KEYBOARD

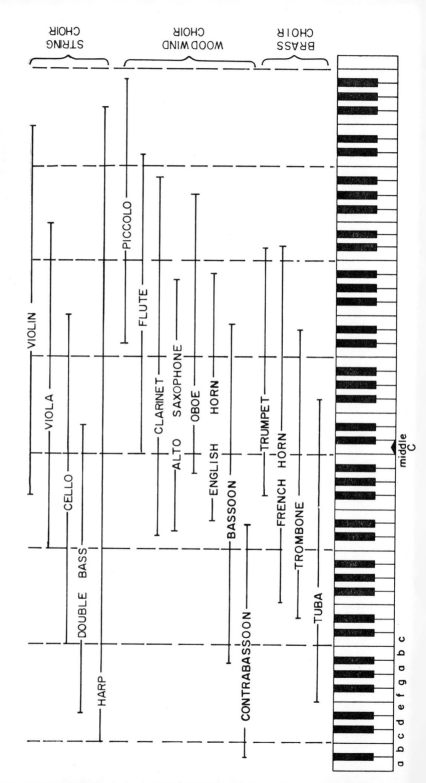

Cello

Viola

Violin

String bass

STRING CHOIR

VIOLIN FAMILY

Many different types of bowed stringed instruments preceded the violin, which did not become a definite type until the latter part of the sixteenth century. The greatest violinmakers of all time lived in Cremona, Italy, during the Baroque period. Most notable of these were Niccolo Amati (1596–1686), Antonio Stradivari (1644–1737), and Giuseppe Bartolomeo Guarneri (1698–1744). The great violinmakers of Cremona also made many very fine violas and cellos. The string bass has retained the sloping shoulders of the viol family, predecessor of the violin family.

9

Harp

String Choir (Continued)

Harps, documented as early as 3000 B.C., through the ages have changed only in size, shape, general appearance, and sound. Structurally they have remained the same, in that the strings are vertical to the soundboard which is at the end of the strings. ¶Early history of the harpsichord is rather obscure. In the fourteenth century, there are evidences of instruments that may be called ancestors of the harpsichord. From that time on until the eighteenth century, many different kinds of similarly sounding keyboard instruments of varying sizes and shapes appeared. The photograph is of a Flemish, seventeenth-century, grand harpsichord, made by one of the Ruckers family and decorated in France, c. 1735.

Harpsichord

Photo, Courtesy H. & A. Selmer, Inc., Elkhart, Indiana

Piccolo   Flute   English Horn   Oboe

WOODWIND CHOIR

The flute is one of the oldest and most widely known instruments. Theobald Boehm (1794–1881) did much to improve the traverse (side-blown) flute. The clarinet first appeared during the latter part of the seventeenth century and was originally made in many sizes to make it easier to play in different keys. The saxophone was invented by Adolphe Sax and patented in 1846. It is made in many sizes but the alto is the commonest. The shawm, ancient ancestor of the oboe, seems to have originated in the Near East about 2800 B.C. Islamic culture aided in its spread in Asia, Africa, and Europe. During the seventeenth century, the French greatly improved it and brought the oboe into being.

Bass clarinet

Soprano clarinet

Alto clarinet

Alto saxophone

Bassoon

¶The bass shawm or early bassoon came into being during the middle of the sixteenth century. The contrabassoon originated during the middle of the eighteenth century. All the instruments of the woodwind choir have been greatly improved since they made their first appearance.

Oboe

BRASS CHOIR

Horns and trumpets date back to prehistoric times when they were made of ram's horns or ox horns. The early metal horns were curved—imitating the shape of the ox horn—or straight. Brass instruments are strictly Western; they were never used in Oriental art music. They went through many stages of development and did not begin to be of musical value until during the sixteenth century.

*Photos, Courtesy,
Conn Corporation,
Elkhart, Indiana*

14

Slide trombone

Trumpet

Cornet

¶Some early brass instruments had side-holes to be covered by the fingers. Not until 1813 were valves invented for brass instruments and, furthermore, composers did not write for them until 1835.

¶Brass instruments have undergone many changes in size and shape. Improvements in metals and design, plus precision manufacturing, have made it possible to manufacture better instruments today than ever before.

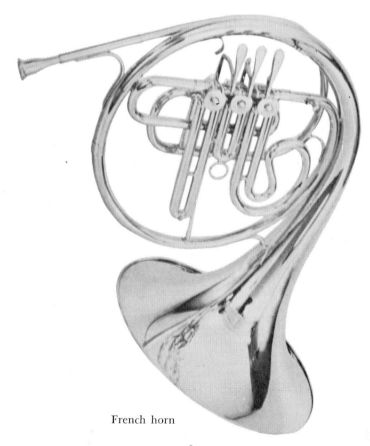

French horn

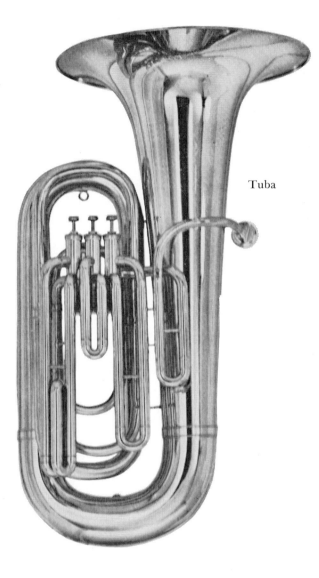

Tuba

PERCUSSION CHOIR

Cymbals

Snare drum

Primitive percussion objects appear to be as old as mankind. The drum, as a specific type, existed in Mesopotamia about 3000 B.C. and in Egypt about 2000 B.C. The earliest Oriental bass drum was probably about five feet in diameter. Through the years it was made smaller until it reached its present size. On the other hand, kettledrums were originally very small and through the years made larger until they reached their present size. The first evidences of a kettledrum are found in Persia, dating c. 600 A.D. A central screw to act on all tuning screws for quick changes of pitch was invented in 1812. The more recent pedal drum can change pitch in a few seconds. There is no proof that the drum, as a musical instrument, appeared in Europe until about 600 A.D.

Cymbals were in existence in India in the fifth century. Their use spread throughout Asia and in Turkey were used more than in any other country. Cymbals were first used as a musical instrument in Europe during the latter part of the seventeenth century.

Haydn's **Military Symphony** (1794) is one of the earliest compositions that includes bass drum, cymbals, and triangle.

Timpani

Bass drum

Photos, Courtesy,
Conn Corporation,
Elkhart, Indiana

General Comparisons

A few general ideas apply to all of the instruments of the orchestra. First, let us consider their size. The smaller they are, the higher the pitch; the larger they are, the lower the pitch. Compare the violin in size with the very low-sounding double bass, the piccolo with the flute, or the trumpet with the trombone. In the string choir the instruments having the longest strings sound the lowest. Likewise, the wind instruments having the longest air column have the lowest pitches.

Next, let us consider the diameter of the wind instruments. The thinner the air column, the more brilliant the timbre. Compare the bass trombone with the tuba. They may both sound the same pitch but the trombone will have a much more brilliant and penetrating quality. In other words, the greater the diameter of the instrument, the more mellow the timbre will be. The bass clarinet looks a great deal like a saxophone but the saxophone has a greater diameter and consequently sounds much more mellow. The saxophone is much more valuable in a band than in an orchestra because its timbre is quite distinct from the other instruments and its mellowness aids in blending the more brilliant instruments.

It is rather easy to learn to identify the flute by its sound because it is like a smooth-sounding whistle. Its little brother, the piccolo, is like a very shrill, high-sounding whistle. The piccolo is the smallest instrument in the orchestra. In the flute family we have the piccolo, the flute, alto flute, and bass flute. These may be called high soprano, soprano, alto, and bass. This family has no reeds. The tone is rather open and clear.

Reeds serve as vibrators for the air columns in the one-reed and two-reed instruments. The timbre of these instruments is referred to as "reedy." The one-reed instruments are the clarinet and the saxophone. The saxophone has a much more mellow quality as explained above. The clarinet family has a soprano, alto, and double bass (sometimes called bass clarinet, pedal clarinet, or contrabass clarinets). The saxophone family is made up of the sopranino (high soprano), soprano, alto, tenor, baritone, and bass.

The oboe family (double reed), made up of the oboe, English horn, bassoon, and contrabassoon, represent soprano, alto, baritone, and bass. They are rather nasal sounding. This quality of timbre is created by the reeds vibrating against each other. The oboe has the most brilliant and penetrating sound. The English horn is much larger than the oboe and has a more mellow timbre. It has a pear-shaped end. The oboe has a thinner air column than the English horn. The bassoon has about the same timbre as the oboe but it seems to be little more mellow sounding because it is pitched much lower. It has a very long tubelike air column which is wrapped around and around, hence the European name for the instrument, fagotto (bundle of sticks). The contrabassoon sounds an octave lower than the bassoon. These two instruments are often called the clowns of the orchestra.

The trumpet and cornet may well be called the soprano of the brass choir. They are the smallest of this group and play the same pitches. The trumpet is more brilliant because it has thinner tubing than the cornet and, because of its brilliance, it is more popular.

The trombone, because of its small diameter, is also brilliant. It has a family of four: tenor, bass, tenorbass, and doublebass. The trombone is actually a bass trumpet.

The French horn is easily recognized because it is the mellowest of the smaller brass instruments. Its tubing is wound around in almost a perfect circle.

The tuba, the largest of all the brass choir, has the greatest diameter of all. It plays the mellow bass parts and has various shapes for various purposes. See Chapter 8, Nineteenth-Century Orchestral Developments, page 71.

We suggest that the listener become familiar with the timbre of the highest sounding and lowest sounding instruments first. After that the middle ranged instruments will be easier to identify.

The percusssion choir is made up of instruments that produce sound when struck. The drums are timpani (kettledrums), bass drum, side, and snare drums. The side and snare drums are the same except the snare drum has snares or wires stretched across one head and is beaten on the other. The side drum has no snares. Everyone is acquainted with the bass drum—the largest and lowest in pitch. The timpani or kettledrums are shaped like half a ball and are tuned to different pitches.

Other percussion instruments are chimes, cymbals (large metal discs), gong (huge suspended metal disc which is struck by a bass drumstick), triangle, glockenspiel or bell lyre (metal bars on a frame shaped like a lyre), castanets, tambourine, celesta (bell-like sounding instrument played from a keyboard like a piano), xylophone (keys of hard wood), marimba (similar to the xylophone but with metal resonating tubes placed beneath the wooden keys), vibraphone (similar to the marimba but with electrically operated vibrators), wind machine (a machine that makes a sound like wind), and all sorts of instruments for sound effects, such as wood-blocks, sand-blocks, and various noise-making devices.

IDENTIFYING INSTRUMENTS
BY THEIR TIMBRE

The Nutcracker Suite by Tchaikovsky is an excellent orchestral suite through which to acquaint yourself with the timbre of the different instruments. It is well to listen for one instrument at a time. The outline given below mentions various instruments where they have important parts.

There are two forms mentioned (see the Glossary for Rondo Form and Ternary Form). As you get better acquainted with this suite you will recognize the ternary form in other places than those mentioned. The ones that are mentioned are easiest to recognize. The same is true of the instruments—you will soon recognize instruments other than those italicized in the outline.

The Nutcracker Suite, Peter Tchaikovsky, Op. 71 a.

1. "Miniature Overture"—*Rondo form* A-B-A-C-A-B-A-C. The "A" melody is played first by the *strings,* the "B" melody by the *flute* and the "C" melody by the *strings.* Listen for the tinkling *triangle* in "A."
2. "March"—Listen for two short tunes, one by the *brass,* the other by the *strings,* punctuated by the *cymbals.* Note that another in the middle section is played by the *flutes.*
3. "Dance of the Sugarplum Fairy"—The *celesta* plays the most important part. At the very beginning it seems to be having a little conversation with the *bass clarinet.*
4. "Trepak"—This is with *full orchestra.* Note the *tambourine.*
5. "Arab Dance"—This is an excellent composition with which to learn to identify the members of the *woodwind choir.* At various times the different members of this choir take the melody. All *strings* are *muted.* A mute is a clasp that is placed on the bridge of a stringed instrument to give it a quiet, sombre, and sort of mysterious effect. The melodies are played by the instruments in this order: *clarinet, muted violins, bassoon, muted violins, clarinet, oboe, English horn, clarinet.* Note that near the end we hear the clarinet, oboe,

and English horn each in turn playing the melody one right after the other.

6. "Chinese Dance"—The first instruments you will hear are the *bassoons*, playing staccato (very short notes). The stringed instruments are played by plucking the strings with the fingers. This is called *pizzicato*. The *flute* has the first melody, a short tune which it repeats immediately. Then the *piccolo* joins the *flute* playing the same sort of tune turned upside down. This is called *inversion*.

7. "Dance of the Toy Flutes"—This is in ternary form (A-B-A). (A) Three *flutes*, a little extra melody by the *English horn*— (B) *Brass choir*, melody by *trumpets*. Listen for the rhythmic pattern played by the *timpani*.

8. "Waltz of the Flowers"—Introduction by the *woodwinds* and *French horn, harp* cadenza (a part played by a solo instrument, usually with considerable technical display), short melody by *French horns*, alternating with short melody by *clarinet, strings* alternating with *woodwind choir*, etc. From here on, try to identify as many instruments as you can.

Suggested Works for the Study of Timbre:

For those who wish to make a further and different study of the timbre of individual instruments and orchestral tone colors, the following works are recommended. The first two of these compositions were written for this purpose. Interesting and enlightening comments are made along with the music. The Britten work deals more thoroughly with individual instruments but also illustrates how they sound as solo instruments in combination with other instruments. The Hanson work deals with individual instruments but devotes more attention to various combinations of instruments and how a composer puts them together to create different orchestral tone colors.

Britten, Benjamin: "Young Person's Guide to the Orchestra" (with narrator)

Hanson, Howard: "The Composer and His Orchestra"— *Merry Mount Suite* (with narrator)

The following list of compositions is for those who wish to make a more extensive study of the timbre of individual instruments. Each instrument listed is followed by the name of a composition for that particular instrument or one in which the instrument has the melody or solo part throughout most of the composition.

Violin: Bach, J. S.: "Sonatas for Violin Alone"
Viola: Berlioz: *Harold in Italy*
Violin and Viola: Mozart: *Sinfonia Concertante,* in E flat, for Violin and Viola
Violoncello: Saint-Saëns: "The Swan," from *Carnival of the Animals*
Violin and Cello: Brahms: Concerto in a minor for Violin and Cello, Op. 102
Double Bass: Saint-Saëns: "The Elephant," from *Carnival of the Animals*
Harp: Boieldieu, François Adrien: Concerto in C Major for Harp
Harpsichord: Scarlatti: "Sonatas for Harpischord"
Piccolo: Vivaldi: Concerti in a minor and C Major for Piccolo
Flute: Bach: "Sonata for Unaccompanied Flute" (BWV 1013)
Clarinet: Mozart: Quintet in A Major for Clarinet and Strings, K. 581
Saxophone: Mussorgsky: *"Il Vecchio Castello,"* from *Pictures at an Exhibition*
Oboe: Telemann: *Concerto for Oboe, String Orchestra and Continuo*
English horn: Sibelius: The Swan of Tuonela, Op. 27, No. 3
Bassoon: Mozart: Concerto in B flat for Bassoon, K. 191
Trumpet: Haydn: Concerto in E flat for Trumpet and Orchestra
French horn: Mozart: *Concerti for French Horn and Orchestra* (4)
Celesta: Tchaikovsky: "Dance of the Sugarplum Fairy," from *The Nutcracker Suite*

Chapter Three

PRE-RENAISSANCE
(600-1400)

MUSIC of the Pre-Renaissance is practically all vocal—monophonic or polyphonic. A single unaccompanied melody is called monophonic. Polyphonic music has two or more melodies played or sung simultaneously. The term "polyphonic" refers preferably to early music.

The Gregorian Chant is the most important music of this period. Although madrigals and motets came into being at this time, the earliest ones of interest to the average listener will be found among those written during the Renaissance.

The Gregorian Chant is a monophonic, liturgical chant of the Roman Catholic Church, named after Pope Gregory (590–604), who collected and standardized the use of chants in the church. The Gregorian Chant, traditionally unaccompanied, has no set rhythm but is more or less oratorical, conforming to the meaning of the text. It is "syllabic" when there is one note to a syllable and "melismatic" when there are two or more notes to a syllable. There are also times when there is recitation on a single tone.

The chants that were added to the Gregorian collection gradually changed and during the thirteenth century became known as plainsongs. Most plainsongs have accompaniments and are rhythmically free, somewhat like the chants. The terms "chant" and "plainsong" (see Glossary) have become synonyms by general usage.

For those who wish to delve into antiquity we suggest Gregorian Chants sung in authentic and traditional manner by groups such as the Benedictine Monks. Recordings are available of practically every type of service: Christmas, Vespers, Easter, Requiems, etc.

Several of the very early religious musical dramas have been quite successfully recreated. Favorite subjects were Christmas, Easter, Herod, Rachel, Pilate, the Flight into Egypt, etc. "The Play of Daniel" by the students of the Cathedral of Beauvais, dated about 1150, is an interesting example.

For those who wish to explore secular music of this period we suggest the music of Adam de la Halle (c. 1240–1287) and Guillaume de Machaut (c. 1300–1377) as starters. Typical titles of secular compositions include ballades, virelais, rondeaux, etc. Antique titles should not be confused with similar contemporary terms.

Suggested Mass of the Middle Ages:

Machaut, Guillaume de (c. 1300–1377): *La Messe de Nostre Dame* (Mass of Our Lady)
> Legend has it that this Mass was written for the coronation of the French King Charles V in 1364. This has since been refuted. It is scored for five singers: soprano, alto, two tenors, and bass. This Mass is a great step forward in composition, signalling the works of the Renaissance. If not the first it is certainly one of the earliest musical settings of the Ordinary of the Mass composed throughout by one composer. Other earlier Masses and some later Masses are known to be based on or made up of various existing tunes, folk songs, and chants. This type of setting of the Mass, based on preexisting musical material, is called a "parody Mass."

Chapter Four

RENAISSANCE
(1400-1600)

MUSIC of the Renaissance may be characterized as being predominantly polyphonic. During this period composers developed what may be termed, according to present-day standards, rational methods of writing. The average listener will enjoy the choral music most of all—the motets, madrigals, chansons, and Masses.

A motet of the Renaissance period may be defined as a polyphonic choral composition with a sacred Latin text, designed to be sung in a sacred service without instrumental accompaniment. Choral works sung without accompaniment are called "a cappella."

During this and some of the following periods, musical terms were used rather loosely but the foregoing definition of a Renaissance motet may be used as a general guide and it is certainly less confusing to the average listener than taking into account all of the exceptions. Some motets are for solo voice, some sound homophonic, a few have secular texts, etc. Later, instruments were added, duplicating vocal parts or merely adding to the polyphonic structure.

A madrigal of the Renaissance period may generally be defined as a polyphonic, unaccompanied, choral composition with a secular text which is sung most often in the mother tongue. The text is usually not serious but in a pastoral, lighthearted or contemplative mood. The two chief sources of madrigals are of Italian and English origin. Some madrigals are accompanied by, or singing parts are duplicated by, instruments of the period. Most of these antique instruments are no longer used except to reproduce this music as authentically as possible. Many exceptions are to be found in the madrigal literature that are similar to some exceptions among motets.

The chanson, or French chanson as it is often called, is predominantly homophonic (melody with accompaniment) but still has some polyphony. Tempi, rhythms, and general character of the music are closely associated with the spirit of the text which is in French. Subjects range from the frivolous to the ordinary with a few being rather serious. For all practical purposes for the listener there is not a great deal of difference between the chanson and the madrigal except in name and language.

The Ordinary is the part of the Mass that remains contant. It contains the *Kyrie, Gloria* (which is omitted during both Advent and Lent), *Credo, Sanctus,* and *Agnus Dei*—the parts of the Mass that are most frequently sung. The *Benedictus* (Blessed is he who cometh in the name of the Lord) and the *Hosanna in Excelsis* (Hosanna in the Highest), often sung, follow the *Sanctus.* The Proper is the part that changes with the church calendar— Christmas, Palm Sunday, Easter, etc.

The Ordinary of the Mass may be translated as follows:

KYRIE

Lord, have mercy upon us.
Christ, have mercy upon us.
Lord, have mercy upon us.

GLORIA

Glory be to God on High, and on earth peace, good will towards men.
We praise thee, we bless thee, we worship thee, we glorify thee,
We give thanks to thee for thy great glory,
O Lord God, heavenly King, God the Father Almighty.
O Lord, the only begotten Son, Jesus Christ;
O Lord God, Lamb of God, Son of the Father,
That takest away the sins of the world, have mercy upon us.
Thou that takest away the sins of the world, receive our prayer.
Thou that sittest at the right hand of God the Father,
Have mercy upon us. For thou only art holy;
Thou only art the Lord; thou only, O Christ, with the Holy Ghost,
Art most high in the glory of God the Father. Amen.

CREDO

I believe in one God the Father Almighty, Maker of heaven and
  earth,
And of all things visible and invisible;
And in one Lord Jesus Christ, the only begotten Son of God;
Begotten of his Father before all worlds,
God of God, Light of Light, Very God of Very God;
Begotten, not made; Being of one substance with the Father;
By whom all things were made:
Who for us men and for our salvation came down from heaven,
And was incarnate by the Holy Ghost of the Virgin Mary,
And was made man: And was crucified also for us under Pontius
  Pilate;
He suffered and was buried:
And the third day he rose again according to the Scriptures:
And ascended into heaven, And sitteth on the right hand of the
  Father:
And he shall come again, with glory, to judge both the quick and
  the dead;
Whose kingdom shall have no end. And I believe in the Holy
  Ghost,
The Lord, and Giver of Life, Who proceedeth from the Father
  and the Son;
Who with the Father and the Son together is worshipped and
  glorified;
Who spake by the Prophets: And I believe one Catholic and
  Apostolic Church:
I acknowledge one Baptism for the remission of sins:
And I look for the Resurrection of the dead:
And the Life of the World to come. Amen.

SANCTUS

Holy, Holy, Holy, Lord God of hosts,
Heaven and earth are full of thy glory:
Glory be to thee, O Lord Most High. Amen.

AGNUS DEI

O Lamb of God, that takest away the sins of the world, have
  mercy upon us.
O Lamb of God, that takest away the sins of the world, have
  mercy upon us.
O Lamb of God, that takest away the sins of the world, grant us
  thy peace.

RENAISSANCE VOCAL MUSIC

The Renaissance music listed here is divided into what is sometimes called Early Renaissance and High Renaissance. The latter extends into the early part of the seventeenth century. Early Renaissance music is given here for those interested in the historical development of music and those explorers who find great pleasure in early music. The average listener will probably find High Renaissance music more attractive to start with.

The lists below suggest specific compositions but aside from this some general suggestions should be pointed out. The motets of John Dunstable (d. 1453) and the chansons of Johannes Ockeghem (1430–1495) are good examples of Early Renaissance music. Interesting vocal forms of the High Renaissance are as follows: Elizabethan madrigals by Thomas Morley (1557–1602) and William Byrd (1543–1623)—Italian madrigals by Carlo Gesualdo (*c.* 1560–1613)—Italian ballads by Giovanni Gastoldi (*c.* 1550–1622)—chansons by Clément Janequin (*c.* 1485–1560) and Claude Le Jeune (1528–1600)—and especially the motets of Orlandus Lassus (1532–1594).

Suggested Early Renaissance Music:

Dufay, Guillaume (*c.* 1400–1474): Mass: *Se la face ay pale*
Isaac, Heinrich (*c.* 1450–1517): Music for the Court of Lorenzo (de' Medici) "the Magnificent"
Josquin des Prés (*c.* 1450–1521): *Missa Pange lingua*
Obrecht, Jacob (1452–1505): Masses: *Sub tuum praesidium* and *Fortuna desperata*

Suggested Music of the High Renaissance:

Byrd, William (1543–1632): Mass for Four Voices and Mass for Five Voices
Gibbons, Orlando (1583–1625): First Short Service
Lassus, Orlandus (1532–1594): Masses: *Puisque j'ai perdu, Bell 'Amfitrit 'Altera,* and *In Die Tribulationis*
Palestrina, Giovanni Pierluigi da (*c.* 1525–1594): *Missa Papae Marcelli*
Sweenlinck, Jan Pieterszoon (1562–1621): Psalms of David
Tallis, Thomas (*c.* 1505–1585): Lamentations of Jeremiah
Victoria, Tomás Luis de (*c.* 1548–1611): *Missa pro Defunctis*

RENAISSANCE INSTRUMENTAL MUSIC

During the middle of the Renaissance period, more and more instrumental music was written down and preserved. By the end of the period, composers had developed instrumental music as an independent medium of musical expression.

Instruments of this period are quite different from our contemporary instruments and even some of those with the same names sound and look quite different. Instruments that were in common use during the Renaissance period are: recorder, flute, shawm, krummhorn, cornett, soprano-fiddle, tenor-fiddle, viola d'amore, viola da gamba, double bass, sackbut, portable organ, clavichord, harpsichord, spinet, virginal, lute, double lute or chitarrone, guitar, vielle, and many others. Some of these instruments were used in connection with vocal music as accompaniment, in unison with vocal parts, or as additions to the polyphonic structure.

Few listeners are interested in Renaissance instrumental music but for those who are, music of the following Elizabethan composers is suggested: John Bull (*c.* 1562–1628), William Byrd (1543–1623), John Dowland (*c.* 1563–1626), Orlando Gibbons (1583–1625), and Thomas Morley (1557–1602). Most interested listeners enjoy the graceful and charming lute and keyboard pieces most of all. If you like early keyboard music do not overlook the "Fitzwilliam Virginal Book," dated 1620, containing nearly 300 compositions written in the late sixteenth and early seventeenth centuries by many different composers. This collection contains dances, preludes, variations, fantasias, and other forms of the period.

The great Venetian master, Giovanni Gabrieli (1557–1612), composed some very interesting music for brass; it was outstanding for the period. See Chapter 13, Music for Wind Instruments.

Jan Pieterszoon Sweelinck (1562–1621) is one of the earliest notable organ composers. His *O Lux Beata Trinitas* (O Light of Blessed Trinity) for pipe organ is a very beautiful and enjoyable composition even according to present-day standards. Don't overlook his Variations on *Mein Junges Leben hat ein End* (My Young Life Has an End), a rather unusual example of an early secular composition for a keyboard instrument—effective and possibly intended for pipe organ.

LISTENING TECHNIQUES

In listening to single melodies, think of them as moving horizontally. Melodies with or without words are musical thoughts. They are speaking to you as if they were phrases, complete sentences, etc. Your response to a musical message may be describable or indescribable. Sometimes you just can't translate your reactions into words. This should not disturb any listener because this is true not only of music but of most other arts.

In listening to polyphonic music, keep in mind again that you are listening to melodies except that you are listening to two or more melodies at the same time. New or repeated tunes, entering at various intervals and at various times, usually begin with considerable emphasis or accent. If you listen for these entrances you will find it rather easy to recognize melodic lines as they appear and reappear. Very often you will find that each voice (soprano, alto, tenor, or bass) will be singing a part that, when heard separately, is a good, expressive melody. In polyphonic music, however, you will find portions that are chordal in structure, i.e., one definite melody supported by harmony.

Chapter Five

BAROQUE
(1600-1750)

WHAT IS BAROQUE MUSIC?

THE TERM "Baroque" (probably derived from the Portuguese word "barroco"—meaning an irregularly shaped pearl) originally implied a sort of excessively grand style in poor taste. A re-evaluation, however, is necessary because music of this period cannot be described as being in poor taste. Most of the arts have adapted the term to indicate the developments that took place during the seventeenth century, and the early part of the eighteenth century.

Baroque music is often polyphonic like that of the Renaissance, but goes a step farther in some cases and becomes "contrapuntal." By "contrapuntal" (which means having counterpoint) we mean that the melodies in the polyphonic structure have distinctive significance. For example, if it were possible to play the melodies of "Star Spangled Banner" and "Marseillaise" simultaneously and have them sound well, that would be "counterpoint."

Homophonic music (music with a single melody, accompanied) became an important part of the literature of the period. These melodies often have great strength and depth of emotional feeling according to Baroque standards. We find great joy expressed in the melody of "My Spirit Be Joyful," from Bach's *Easter Cantata*, No. 146, and great sorrow expressed in the melody of *"Crucifixus,"* from his Mass in b minor.

A melody in Baroque instrumental music has the same strength of character that is found in vocal music. It is often "discussed" to quite some length. That is to say, the melody is not repeated over and over again identically, but changes somewhat, yet retains the same general character or spirit throughout a section of a composition or throughout the entire piece.

Compositions by leading composers of this period have regular rhythm, ranging from delicate accents in harpsichord music to a strong driving rhythm in orchestral compositions and large vocal works such as the "Hallelujah Chorus" from Handel's *Messiah*. Many Baroque compositions have what may be called "terraced dynamics"—the sudden shifting back and forth from one level of loudness to another.

Baroque music, according to present-day standards, has considerable grandeur and majestic beauty. Practically all the music is serious and certainly it is never sentimental.

It is difficult to characterize vocal music because we cannot help being influenced by the words. This is true particularly of emotional qualities. In polyphonic vocal music we often hear two or more sets of words going on at the same time and this tends to confuse the less experienced listener. If this is true of your listening, try ignoring all word lines except one or just think in terms of the meaning of the text. (See Renaissance Listening Techniques.)

As a guide, the following may be considered an outline of the general characteristics of all Baroque music, but more especially Baroque instrumental music:

1. primarily serious
2. polyphonic and homophonic
3. clear, distinct, well-defined melodies
4. strong to bold, driving, regular rhythm
5. considerable grandeur and majestic beauty

If you know more or less what to expect of music, you will be a little better prepared to enjoy it. The following discussions of the different kinds of Baroque music are designed to act as a guide for that purpose. Baroque music for wind instruments is listed in Chapter 13, Music for Wind Instruments.

BAROQUE INSTRUMENTAL MUSIC

The Baroque Orchestra

The Baroque orchestra was made up of a mixture of ancient instruments and those that were like or similar to those used today. Some instruments used in the orchestra during this period

33

have since been discarded. Various antiquated stringed instruments were more or less duplicates in timbre. Besides the string choir there were very few other instruments. These were very different from each other in timbre—e.g., flute, oboe, and trumpet.

The orchestral compositions of this period lack "color" as we think of it today. Although there is a great deal of homophonic music, the general style of writing was polyphonic. The composers took advantage of the instruments available that varied in timbre by using them to bring out the melodic lines of the polyphonic structure. In other words, two melodies, one by the flute and another by an oboe, going on at the same time, are easy to follow because of the difference in the timbre of the two instruments.

The typical Baroque orchestra was made up of some or all of the following instruments.

String Choir	Woodwind Choir	Brass Choir	Percussion
Violino Piccolo	Flute	Trumpet	Drum
Violin	Recorder	Horn	Kettledrums
Viola	Oboe		
Violoncello	Bassoon		
Double bass			
Harpsichord			

The string choir is the most important group of instruments in the Baroque orchestra. It predominates in most orchestral compositions and in many it is used alone.

The violino piccolo is like a small violin but tuned higher. It has much less volume than the other stringed instruments. Its timbre may be described as being like a slightly muted violin and a bit nasal.

Some Baroque flutes had keys, others were without them. Keys for the flute were invented in 1677.

The recorder is an end-blown instrument sounding somewhat like a flute but with a slightly reedy quality. It played an important part in the music of the Renaissance. It was used very little after 1750 and its present-day revival is for those who wish to hear Baroque music as it was originally played.

The kettledrums were not used very often in orchestral compositions, but were used often in festival and ceremonial music.

Of course we have the age-old question which has no answer,

"Would a Baroque composer have used other kinds of instruments had they been available?" Many Baroque compositions are played and also recorded on modern instruments. These recordings have merit and are worth investigating.

The Baroque Suite

The typical Baroque suite—whether for one, two, or three or more instruments—is made up of a group of antique dances. The interest is sustained through variety. One unifying element is that all the dances or movements are often in the same key. Sometimes, as in all the Bach suites for orchestra, the first number is an overture. In Handel's *Royal Fireworks Suite,* the overture was intended as a greeting to the royal visitors. (See Chapter 13, Music for Wind Instruments.)

Bach was not an innovator, but when he set out to work in any established form, his compositions always seemed to surpass in quality those of his predecessors or contemporaries.

In his suites for orchestra, he not only amalgamated previous styles but gave them fine melodies along with solid harmonic and polyphonic texture. These are the characteristics that are quite largely responsible for their continued success. They are perennial favorites with learned and unlearned alike.

Suggested Baroque Suites for Orchestra:

Bach: *Suite No. 3 for Orchestra* (see Ballet, page 77)
   Overture, Air, Gavotte, Bourrée, Gigue.
   Scored for 3 trumpets, drums, 2 oboes, violins I and II, viola, violoncello, and harpsichord.
Bach: *Suite No. 4 for Orchestra*
   Overture, Bourrée, Gavotte, Menuetto, Rejouissance.
   Scored for 3 trumpets, drums, 3 oboes, 2 bassoons, violins I and II, viola, and violoncello.
Handel: *Water Music*
   The complete suite is made up of twenty-two short numbers. There is great variety in tempo and instrumentation. Handel uses many different combinations of strings, brass, and woodwinds in the various movements which include some seventeenth-century dances.

The Baroque Solo Concerto

The Baroque solo concerto is a composition with considerable polyphonic treatment, written for a solo instrument and orchestra. In its strictest sense it is not a solo with accompaniment but a composition with a unified feeling of teamwork between orchestra and solo instrument—a "working together."

Most Baroque solo concerti are in three or four movements. The movements generally alternate from fast to slow. The pattern of the three-movement concerto favored by Bach is fast-slow-fast. Giuseppe Torelli (1658–1709) was the first to introduce the solo concerto and one of the very first to compose in concerto grosso (see Glossary) style.

The solo concerto is one of the easiest instrumental types of the period for the listener because his attention is continually being focused on the solo instrument. Listening to a solo concerto is an easy way to get acquainted with the timbre of the solo instrument. Note that the suggested list includes six different solo instruments.

Suggested Baroque Solo Concerti:

Bach: Violin Concerto No. 2 in E Major
Bach: Harpsichord Concerto in D Major (above concerto transcribed)
Corelli: Concerto for Oboe and String Orchestra
Handel: Concerti for Pipe Organ and Chamber Orchestra, Op. 4 (6) and Op. 7 (6)
Pergolesi: Concerto in G Major for Flute and String Orchestra
Torelli: Concerti for Trumpet, Strings, and Continuo
Vivaldi: Concerto in b minor for Violin, Strings, and Harpsichord
Vivaldi: *The Four Seasons* (Four Concerti for Violin and String Orchestra)
These are named "Spring," "Summer," "Autumn," and "Winter." They are outstanding examples of early program music (see Glossary).

Suggested Baroque Concerti for Two Solo Instruments:

Bach: Concerto in d minor for Two Violins and String Orchestra
Torelli: Concerto Op. 8, No. 2 in a minor for Two Violins, String Orchestra, and Harpsichord
Torelli: Concerto for Violin and Guitar (or Lute) and Orchestra
This is actually a violin concerto with concertino section (see Glossary) played by the solo violin and guitar. A delightful and unusual composition.
Vivaldi: Concerto in G Major for Two Guitars (or Lutes) and String Orchestra

The slow movement by the two guitars alone is exquisitely charming.

Vivaldi: Concerto in d minor for Two Violins and Orchestra

Suggested Baroque Concerti for Three Solo Instruments:

Bach: Concerto in a minor for Harpsichord, Flute, Violin, and String Orchestra
The slow movement is played by the solo instruments without the orchestra.

Bach: Concerto in C Major for Three Harpsichords and Orchestra
A magnificent work—exceptionally appealing to those interested in harpsichord music.

Vivaldi: Concerto in F Major for Three Violins and Orchestra

The Baroque Concerto Grosso

The typical Baroque concerto grosso differs from the solo concerto in that there is a *group* of solo instruments against the full orchestra which is made up primarily or entirely of strings. The solo group is called "concertino" and the entire orchestra is called "tutti" or "ripieno."

There is considerable "conversation" between the solo group and the whole orchestra—sometimes the solo group, or one of them, will be heard alone—sometimes the main orchestral body will be heard by itself—then at times all the solo instruments and the orchestra will be playing at the same time. Many sudden changes in dynamics are typical, and many extended passages in the same volume are to be found.

Suggested Baroque Concerti Grossi:

Bach: Brandenburg Concerto No. 5 (String Orchestra with Flute, Violin, and Harpsichord as concertino)
The second movement is for the concertino alone.

Corelli: Concerti Grossi, Op. 6 (12)
Number 8 in this opus is the well-known "Christmas Concerto."

Handel: Concerti Grossi, Op. 6 (12)

Pergolesi: Concertino in f minor for String Orchestra, No. 4

Torelli: Sinfonia in D Major (Giegling 29)

Torelli: Sinfonia in D Major (Giegling 31)
These two sinfonias by Torelli are actually in concerto grosso style although named "sinfonias." Giegling, in editing the compositions of Torelli, assigned numbers to the compositions to aid in identifying them.

The Baroque Sonata

The term "sonata" has more meanings than any other term in all music history. It appeared well over four hundred years ago and its meaning has been changing ever since. Its meaning depends upon how and when it was used. The term "sonata" and practically all other terms designating Baroque forms were not standardized or uniform in meaning.

A Baroque sonata is for one or more instruments and has one or more movements. Many times these sonatas are scored for antique instruments such as some of those listed under instrumental music of the Renaissance. The average listener may find recordings played by contemporary instruments more palatable.

The "Trio Sonata" *(sonata a trè)* is an important instrumental form of chamber music of the Baroque period. The term "trio," like the term "sonata," had many meanings, also depending upon how and when it was used. The typical trio sonata was written for two instruments having melodic importance and a continuo. The continuo is for a keyboard instrument—most often for a harpsichord but sometimes for a pipe organ. The continuo fills in the harmonic or polyphonic structure according to certain rules too technical to be of value here. Very often a cello or viola da gamba is added to play along with the keyboard instrument, duplicating the bass part. Thus the so-called trio sonata is most often played by four instruments instead of three as we would normally assume from the title.

Since composers, like Bach for instance, were not purists but very practical because of the great demands made upon them in their respective positions, trio sonatas were often written so that they could be played on any group of instruments that was compatible. For example the Trio Sonata in C Major for two violins and continuo, by Bach, has been very effectively played and recorded by flute, oboe, and harpsichord. This combination can produce a superb performance. After getting acquainted with Baroque music, everyone should give the Trio Sonatas a chance. When well played they are most interesting and delightful.

Two types of Baroque sonatas are "sonata da chiesa" (church sonata) and "sonata da camera" (chamber sonata). The idealized chiesa type is in four movements, slow-fast-slow-fast, and is intended for use in church services. The camera type is much more flexible in structure. Sometimes it has more than four movements and sometimes it has fewer than four. Antique dances often appear in the camera type which was intended as salon music for small audiences.

As far as the general characteristics of the music itself are concerned, there is, for the most part, little difference between the chiesa and camera types. Both have slow, stately movements and both have dancelike movements. However, in the chiesa or church sonata the movements are not usually given dance names.

Chamber music was intended to be played in small rooms, not huge auditoriums. By means of recordings you can hear this kind of intimate music in your own home with surroundings as originally intended. The Baroque instruments used in chamber music are generally lighter in volume than concert instruments of today.

Suggested Baroque Sonatas:

Bach: "Sonatas for Flute and Harpsichord" (BWV—1020, 1030, 1031, 1032)

Bach: "Sonatas for Flute and Continuo" (BWV—1033, 1034, 1035)

Bach understood the technical and musical possibilities of the flute. These beautiful sonatas are evidence of his love for the instrument. They have not all been authenticated as being written by Bach but they are beautiful no matter who wrote them.

Bach: Sonata in a minor for Unaccompanied Flute

This is actually not a sonata but a suite of four dances: Allemande, Corrente, Sarabande, and Bourrée Anglaise. This is an illustration of how loosely Bach himself used the term sonata.

Bach: "Trio Sonatas" (4)

Most often played by two violins and continuo but sometimes by other compatible instruments.

Corelli: Sonata, *La Follia,* Op. 5 No. 12 in d minor for Violin and Continuo (Theme and 23 Variations)

Corelli: Trio Sonatas, Op. 3 (12) and Op. 4 (12)

The Fugue

A fugue is a contrapuntal composition with a certain number of tunes called subjects—usually three or four. The main subject is introduced in one position (either soprano, alto, tenor, or bass) and then appears in another, while a second subject is played with it. At the end of this a third subject may be added, and so on, according to certain rules.

The beginning of Johann Sebastian Bach's Fugue in g minor from the Fantasia and Fugue in g minor (The Great) for organ is outlined below. The numbers represent the subjects and show the positions where they are heard.

```
1. - - - - - -   2. * * * * * *   3. # # # # # #   4. ' ' ' ' ' '
                 1. - - - - - -   2. * * * * * *   3. # # # # # #
                                  1. - - - - - -   2. * * * * * *
                                                   1. - - - - - -
```

In this fugue, the first tune that you hear is the main subject, or subject number one. When this is finished, a second subject starts in where the first one left off, and the first one starts again, but this time it is below the second subject as an alto part. When the third subject is added, subject number one becomes the tenor; the second subject becomes the alto and subject number three is the new soprano, etc.

The entire section outlined above is the first exposition of this fugue. Any section of a fugue, in which the main subject appears in all positions or voices, is called an exposition.

The following is an outline of the exposition of the Little Fugue in g minor. Compare this with the exposition of the Great Fugue in g minor outlined above.

```
1. - - - - - -   2. * * * * * *   3. # #         4. ' '
                 1. - - - - - -   2. * * * * * *   3. # #
                                  1. - - - - - -   2. * * * * * *
                                                   1. - - - - - -
```

It is easy to understand the pattern of the exposition of the Great Fugue because it conforms to a regular plan. However, it is easier to follow the Little Fugue in g minor when listening to it. In the Little Fugue we have a feeling of the same sort of exposition that we have above, except that it has but two important tunes or subjects, a main subject and a secondary one. The places where subjects 3 and 4 appear in the Great Fugue are filled with less important tunes. These drop out after a short time. These tunes are polyphonic ideas, added to help make the two subjects more like a part of a greater drama, with more characters, than like a play with but two characters.

First expositions in fugues do not always follow this scheme. Part of the pattern may be inverted, shortened, augmented, or numerous other changes made. All expositions are similar in that the main subject appears successively in all the positions or voices.

Some sections of the fugue are made up of different polyphonic melodies. These episodes, or connecting passages, add variety and new interest. They also help tie the subjects together just as secondary actors in a play help tie together the main activities of the plot.

Listening to Fugues

In listening to a fugue, the most important parts to get acquainted with are the main subject and the first exposition. If a fugue is well played the main subject will be easy to recognize and follow as it appears from time to time. It is not always present any more than the main character in a play is always present. It may not always be played in full—only parts or fragments of it may appear here and there.

As you get a little better acquainted with the main subject of any fugue, you will be able to hear another melody that is being played while the main one is going on. Listen to two simultaneous melodies as you would look at two pictures printed from a film with a double exposure. After you are able to hear two or more melodies at once, you will find it much easier to listen to and enjoy other fugues that you do not know or do not know as well.

An organist usually chooses registrations made up of different timbres such as strings, flutes, oboes, etc., so that he may bring out melodic lines clearly and distinctly. Once you become well acquainted with a fugue you will find that the "mental gymnastics" required to follow the subjects become easier and listening to them becomes fascinating.

Suggested Baroque Organ Fugues (in this order for the beginner):

Bach: Little Fugue in g minor
Bach: Toccata and Fugue in d minor
Bach: Fantasia and Fugue in g minor (The Great)
Bach: Prelude in Fugue in E flat Major (St. Anne)

Miscellaneous Baroque Organ Music

Practically every Baroque organist wrote chorale preludes. The term "chorale" is an old Reformation term given to a song to be sung by the church congregation in the language of the people. A "chorale prelude" is an organ composition based on the tune of a chorale. Familiar chorale preludes are Bach's "Now Thank We All Our God" and "A Mighty Fortress Is Our God."

There are many different kinds of chorale preludes. Some present the melodies unaltered with interesting and varied accompaniments, others are almost like variations, and others seem to hide the melody with a great deal of polyphonic material.

Sometimes these chorale preludes are used at the very beginning of the church service and lead directly into the congregational singing of the same chorale. They were originally designed for this purpose and to acquaint the congregation with the hymn of the day. This idea of the chorale prelude was not new but rather a perfected form or outgrowth of the earlier organ Latin hymns, developed under the auspices of the Roman Catholic Church.

In the hands of Bach the chorale prelude as well as many other Baroque forms—especially the fugue—reached their highest state of development. Of all the composers who preceded Bach, Buxtehude is the most mature according to our present-day perspective of Baroque organ music but all the composers listed here are important in the development of organ literature.

The Baroque "toccata" is a keyboard composition in free style in the idiom of the instrument for which it was written. The term "toccata" was used very loosely. The toccata style was often used as a prelude to a fugue.

"Chaconne" and "passacaglia" are terms that were used interchangeably by seventeenth-century composers and in many respects the listener need not be concerned about their differences. The "chaconne" has a "ground bass" which is normally used as a basis for harmonic structure. The "passacaglia" has a "ground bass" which usually is in the bass but may appear in any other voice. The ground bass is a rather short bass melodic line that is repeated over and over with different harmonic structure and upper melodies for each repetition—often erroneously called "variations."

Much of the early Baroque organ music, like many other types of early music, is primarily for the connoisseur. The way to overcome that handicap is to listen to Baroque music and you will automatically become a connoisseur. You will find it well worthwhile. The listings here are intended to be helpful in locating some of the more interesting and enjoyable examples of different types of Baroque organ music. Since composers of the period used titles rather loosely, a brief explanation is given with most of the numbers suggested for listening.

Suggested Miscellaneous Baroque Organ Music:

Bach: A German Organ Mass (1739)
 This is the third part of the *Clavierübung*. It might well be called a cycle of "chorale preludes," a musical interpretation of the doctrines of the Lutheran Church. This is not actually an Organ Mass but in its entirety contains many chorale preludes—some very simple, some in a very grand style on the same tune or subject—on the catechism and hymns of the church. It is one of the most magnificent "collections" of chorale preludes for organ. It begins with a Prelude followed by various chorale preludes glorifying the Trinity, The Ten Commandments, Faith, The Lord's Prayer, Baptism, Penitence, and The Lord's Supper, ending with a fugue.

Bach: Passacaglia and Fugue in c minor

Bach: "The Schübler Chorales" (Chorale Preludes)

Buxtehude: Prelude, Fugue, and Chaconne in C Major
 The music of Buxtehude changed very little in the course of his lifetime. Although in good Baroque style, it is full of the unexpected—quite like improvising at times. This gives his music a freshness and a distinction from other composers of the period. None of Buxtehude's autographed copies is in existence—only copies of his music made by other people have been discovered.

Frescobaldi: *Toccata per l'Elevatione*
 This is from a collection of organ pieces, *Fiori Musicali* (Musical Flowers). This type of toccata is played during the Mass at the time of the Elevation of the Host. Some of the other pieces from *Fiori Musicali* were intended to be included in the Mass, some probably to be played during the partaking of the sacrament, and others to fill in at various times during the service.

Pachelbel: *Ein' feste Burg ist unser Gott*
 This is an outstanding example of a chorale prelude on "A Mighty Fortress Is Our God." Practically every organist of the period wrote a chorale prelude on this tune.

Scheidt: *Warum Betrubst Du Dich, Mein Herz?*
 "Why art thou restless, O my soul?" is a set of twelve vari-

43

ations. It is from the collection of organ pieces which the composer called *"Tabulatura Nova."*

Walther: *Concerto del Sigr. Meck*

This is an adaptation of a concerto grosso for orchestra by Joseph Meck. Walther arranged it for organ in such a way that he preserved the concerto grosso style and also made it into a very attractive organ composition.

Harpsichord Music

Although the piano in its earliest stages of development was in existence during the Baroque period it is not to be considered a Baroque instrument. Most of the keyboard compositions of the period were written with the harpsichord in mind—not the piano. The suggested numbers that follow are available on records, played on either the harpsichord or the piano.

The "suite" was a favorite among composers who wrote music for the harpsichord. These suites are made up of antique dances such as some of the following: allemande, courante, bourrée, minuet, gavotte, gigue, and passepied. Some include an "air." This is a rather slow melodic piece which often appeared in the French ballet during the seventeenth and eighteenth centuries. The "air" was not in any particular form such as the dances listed above but just music to accompany a dance.

Suggested Baroque Harpsichord Music:

Bach: "Chromatic Fantasy and Fugue"

Bach: Italian Concerto in F Major

The title here is misleading. It is not a concerto for solo instrument and orchestra but for harpsichord alone.

Bach: *Partita* (suite) No. 1 in B flat

A delightful suite made up of a prelude and antique dances.

Bach: *Well-tempered Clavier*

A set of forty-eight preludes and fugues in different keys— each major and minor key being represented twice.

Handel: Suite No. 5 in E Major

This contains the well-known "Harmonious Blacksmith," a theme and variations.

Purcell: *Harpsichord Suites*

Good examples of English Baroque style and "flavor."

BAROQUE CEREMONIAL MUSIC

The purpose of ceremonial music written for nobility during the Baroque period was to add to the pomposity of the court.

King Louis XV of France loved brass fanfares sounding at his every move. Special music was written and played to awaken him in the morning, to announce his entry at all functions, to dine by, to dance to, etc. Some composers spent much time and effort vying with each other for his favor. Some were so expert at writing this kind of music that their reputation spread. As a result, some of them received commissions to write music for special occasions from courts and noblemen outside France.

George II, King of England, was also a great patron of the arts. George Frederick Handel was a great favorite of his, to the exclusion of virtually all other composers.

Although written for ceremonial purposes some of this literature is outstanding.

Suggested Ceremonial Music:

Charpentier: *Epithalamium* (Wedding-Cantata)
A commissioned work written for the marriage of the Duke of Bavaria and the daughter of the King of Poland "in Praise of His Serene Electoral Highness Maximilian Emanuel, Duke of Bavaria."

Charpentier: *Marche de Triomphe*
This was written for Louis XIV for a "carousel" or horse ballet at Versailles.

Gilles: *Requiem*
The orchestral accompaniment, especially the timpani, gives this Requiem an unusual atmosphere of ceremonial dignity. It ranges from the simple devotional to the dramatic and at times is a little pompous. It is typical of French Baroque ceremonial music. It was performed for the funeral services of Jean Philippe Rameau (1764) and His Majesty King Louis XV (1774).

Handel: *Zadok the Priest*
This is one of the anthems written for the coronation of King George II (1727). A brilliant expression of splendid grandeur, it was performed during the anointing of the King with consecrated oil. It has been performed at every coronation since. The text is derived from I Kings 1:38–39.

Lalande, de: "Symphonies for the King's Suppers"
These are suites of short pieces which were played for the King of France while he was dining.

Lully: *Fanfares for the King's Tournament of 1686*
A suite—Grand Prelude, Menuet, Gavotte, Gigue.

45

Lully: *Plaude, laetare Gallia* (1668)

This motet was written for the baptism of the Dauphin (eldest son of the king of France). It is made up of choral, duet, and solo parts. The tenor solo part *"O Jesu vita credentium"* and the chorus that follows are dignified, prayerful, and impressive.

Mouret: *Suites des Symphonies*

These are suites of fanfares and dances.

BAROQUE VOCAL MUSIC
The Baroque Cantata

There is no "typical" Baroque cantata. They are made up of various vocal forms—choruses, solos, duets, etc. Some may be made up entirely of choruses, others made up entirely of solos. Some choruses may be in four-part harmony like a hymn while others are in polyphonic style. Some solo parts are easy to sing, others are very difficult and require considerable vocal training. Most Baroque cantatas have chamber orchestra accompaniments.

Bach wrote about three hundred church cantatas. The texts in most of the approximately two hundred sacred cantatas that remain in existence today are appropriate for particular Sundays of the year, such as Advent, Christmas, Epiphany, Lent, Palm Sunday, Easter, etc. The Sunday services of Bach's time were very long. They thought nothing of having a cantata every Sunday. In fact, preparing a different cantata for every Sunday of the year was required of Bach in his position in Leipzig where he was organist and director of music at Thomaskirche and Nicolaikirche. Some of these cantatas are long but most of them average about twenty-five minutes in length.

Bach's devotion to his church and his firm belief in Christianity are reflected in his church cantatas. He was a firm believer in the redemption of the world through Christ's sacrifice on the cross. In listening to Bach's cantatas the theological aspect should always be considered. Note the sincerity, enthusiasm, and the depth of feeling in the music.

For the most part, texts of cantatas are on religious subjects but a few are secular.

Suggested Church Cantatas:

Bach: Cantata No. 4 (Easter) *Christ lag in Todesbanden* (Christ Lay in Death's Shroud)

Bach: Cantata No. 80, *Ein' feste Burg ist unser Gott* (A Mighty Fortress Is Our God)

Buxtehude: *Das neugenborne Kinderlein* (The Little New-born Child) and *In dulci jubilo* (In Sweet Joy)

These two very short Christmas cantatas (actually not cantatas when compared with others listed here) are in the jolly spirit that one expects in old Christmas carols.

Buxtehude: Cantata *Ihr Lieben Christen fruet euch nun* (Beloved Christians, Now Rejoice)

This cantata, probably intended for All Saints' Day or the last Sunday after Trinity, is made up of two sinfonias, four chorales, a song for solo voice, and an extended Amen after the third chorale.

Suggested Secular Cantatas:

Bach: Cantata No. 211, *Schweiget stille, plaudert nicht* (Coffee Cantata)

Bach: Cantata No. 212, *Mer hahn en neue Oberkeet* (Peasant Cantata)

These two cantatas are delightful examples of the human, lighthearted side of the composer. Too often we think only of the serious side of this great man.

The Oratorio

The oratorio is a much more pretentious work than the cantata. It is very much longer, usually with a religious story or libretto, made up of choruses, solos, and duets with orchestral accompaniment. Like the cantata it is designed to be sung without costumes, scenery, or action, in a church (but not a part of the service) or concert hall.

Suggested Baroque Oratorios:

Bach: *Christmas Oratorio* (1734)

Throughout this oratorio the listener is aware of the Christmas spirit. This is Bach, the father of a large family, expressing his delight and joy at the coming of the Lord and all that Christmastide meant to his family. For example the alto solo "Sleep Thou, My Dearest" is one of the sweetest lullabies ever written and the chorus "Let us even go now to Bethlehem" is very descriptive, portraying the feeling of interest and haste. Each of the six cantatas that comprise this oratorio is devoted to an event or a part of the Christmas season.

Carissimi: *Jepthe* (1650) (in Latin)

This rather short oratorio is a story from the Old Testament about Jepthe's vow to sacrifice to God the first member of his household that he will meet upon his successful return from a battle against the Ammonites.

Handel: *Judas Maccabaeus* (1746) (in English)

Judas Maccabaeus, chosen leader of the Jews, carries out the plan of his deceased father, Mattathias, to deliver his people from the cruelties and oppressions of the Syrians. This oratorio was written in celebration of the success of the Duke of Cumberland in his efforts to suppress any attempted restoration of the Stuarts to the throne of England. Much of it is cast in operatic style and contains some of Handel's finest vocal works.

Handel: *Messiah* (1742) (in English)

This well-known oratorio has a libretto adapted from the Old and New Testaments concerning the coming and life of our Lord.

Schütz: *Christmas Oratorio* (1664) (in German)

This is done on a rather large scale for its time—one of the great vocal works of the seventeenth century. It is made up of "scenes" or narratives by solo voice in recitative style with continuo and choruses with orchestra in "concertato style"— quite dramatic.

Schütz: *Easter Oratorio* (1623) (in German)

The full title of this oratorio is "History of the Resurrection of Jesus Christ." It is an excellent example of the simpler style of early Baroque. It leaves you with the feeling that the composer approached his subject with a pious attitude of sincerity and reverence.

The Baroque Motet

Baroque motets are not like Renaissance motets. They are much longer, being made up of any or all of the following: choruses, solos, duets, trios, etc., with either orchestral or organ accompaniment, or both. Some are in parts while others are continuous. Polyphony is common but there is a great deal of solo and homophonic material in the Baroque motet. They are all very easily comprehended.

Suggested Baroque Motets:

Bach: *Jesu, meine Freude*

This is probably the best known of Bach's six motets.

Campra: *Ecce Panis Angelorum*

This motet is in four parts: 1. *"Ecce Panis Angelorum"*

(tenor solo), 2. *"Venite Adoremus"* (trio—two tenors and baritone), 3. *"Adorate"* (tenor solo), 4. *"Cantate Domino"* (chorus, soloists). The text of each is from a different part of the Bible.

Charpentier: *Oculi Omnium in te sperant*
The text is derived from Psalm 144. This motet is thought to have been written to follow the Benediction of the Most Blessed Sacrament. The spirituality of the music is befitting this place after the service.

Monteverdi: *Psalm Beatus vir* (Blessed is the man that feareth the Lord; he hath great delight in His commandments.)

Baroque Opera

Opera had its beginning during the Baroque period. Both music and the secular drama had to advance before a satisfactory union of these two arts could take place. Prior to this period, music was not sufficiently developed emotionally to bear the burden of the artistic demands of such a combination. There were musical shows centuries before but none worthy of the name of opera.

In general, the emotional content of the music in the earliest operas is limited by logic yet not without depth of expression. The operas are done in a grand style but without flagrant pretense.

Suggested Baroque Operas:

Monteverdi: *L'Incoronazione di Poppea* (1642)
Purcell: *Dido and Aeneas* (1689)

Miscellaneous Baroque Vocal Compositions

For the most part, the suggested list of miscellaneous Baroque vocal music includes only long or major works. The curious and interested listener may find some of the shorter works very much worth investigating. Among these the following should be mentioned: anthems, canticles, hymns, and especially the Psalms of David. Henry Purcell (*c.* 1659–1695), Heinrich Schütz (1585–1672), Jean Joseph Mouret (1682–1738), and Pierre Gautier (1643–1697) are among the composers not mentioned in the suggested list who, nevertheless, should not be overlooked.

49

Suggested Miscellaneous Baroque Vocal Compositions:

Bach: Mass in b minor

Bach: *St. Matthew Passion*

> Both the Mass in b minor and the *St. Matthew Passion* are very long monumental choral works that rank with the finest vocal literature of all time. The *St. Matthew Passion* is a musical setting of the apostle's account of the crucifixion of the Lord.

Campra: Requiem

> The composer, an ecclesiastic, presents the spiritual aspects of the Requiem with reverence. It is a sincere musical expression of faith.

Campra: *Te Deum*

> From the simple devotional to the operatic and at times pompous approach, Campra turned out a musical setting—in grand style—of this fourth-century text by St. Ambrose of Milan.

Charpentier: *Te Deum*

> The composer makes the most of the text, running the gamut of emotional expression with great orchestral and vocal coloring. Charpentier composed six exciting settings of the *Te Deum.*

Charpentier: Midnight Mass

> The text of the Mass is set to the tunes of Christmas Carols in this most unusual Mass for the Christmas midnight service. The delightful orchestral and organ interludes and accompaniment enhance the beauty and spirit of this seldom-heard Christmas Mass.

Handel: Dettingen *Te Deum* and *Jubilate* (1743)

> Although not authenticated as a completely original work, this is a great masterpiece of vocal music. It was written in celebration of the victory of the British forces over the French.

Lalande, de: *Te Deum*

> This setting of the canticle of praise to God is a good example of French Baroque choral music—rather long and grandiose but enriched with variety—conforming to the various aspects of the text from quiet moods to thrilling, dramatic praise.

Monteverdi: *Madrigali Guerrier ed Amorosi* (Madrigals of War and Love)

> This is an early Baroque set of madrigals which might well

be called a "madrigal-cycle." They run the gamut of emotion from tender love to a robust call to arms. A masterpiece in contrasting dramatic moods, done in "concertato style" (intentionally pitting vocal or instrumental parts against each other). It is made up of solos, duets, and trios with continuo, choruses, and orchestra.

Monteverdi: *Messa a 4 Voice da Cappella*

This Mass is composed in the style of the Renaissance except that the score calls for an instrumental bass (organ) which doubles the lowest voice but occasionally is an independent part. It was probably written for St. Mark's Cathedral in Venice where Monteverdi was *Maestro da Cappella* from 1613 until he died in 1643.

Scheidt: *Magnificat Noni Toni (Magnificat Anima Mea Dominum)*

This Magnificat, "My soul doth magnify the Lord," is an excellent example of the practice of the period which is still continued in some churches, especially in Europe. The organ is substituted for the choir in the alternate verses of Psalms, canticles, and hymns. If you are interested in early church music don't miss this treasure.

Vivaldi: Gloria in D Major

This magnificent composition is one of the most easily comprehended choral works of the period. It is written for solo voices, chorus, and orchestra—a rather long, glorious setting of this part of the Mass.

Chapter Six

ROCOCO AND PRE-CLASSIC
(1700-1775)

DURING the eighteenth century, delicate ornamentation emphasizing elegance appeared in paintings, furniture, chandeliers, etc. This movement in the arts became known as "Rococo," a term derived from the French word "Rocaille," which means shell or shellwork.

Rococo music is a sort of transition between the Baroque and the Classic art of Haydn, Mozart, and the early compositions of Beethoven. It is a departure from the grandeur of the Baroque emphasizing simplicity. Rococo composers wrote music that was basically graceful and charming with qualities of prettiness, pleasantness, and elegance.

This transitional period may also be called Pre-Classic—a period during which the style and form of music of many composers was in a very fluid state, retaining some characteristics of the past but leaning toward a new style that was later to be known as Classic. Many composers in this category were neither true Baroque nor true Classic according to our present-day point of view.

Polyphonic music of the Baroque period was being replaced with music that was primarily homophonic. The Baroque concerto grosso was giving way to the Classic symphony and various forms were contributing to the development of the Classic sonata form (see Chapter 7).

J. W. A. Stamitz (1717–1757) must be mentioned here—not because of his compositions, but because of his contributions to music and his influence on others, notably Haydn and Mozart. At the court of Mannheim, under his leadership, the Mannheim School explored the possibilities and uses of a long crescendo (gradual increasing in volume), the diminuendo (gradual decreasing in volume) and various shadings to make music more expressive.

Although Franz Joseph Haydn (1732–1809) and Wolfgang Amadeus Mozart (1756–1791) are recognized as Classicists, some of their early and more youthful compositions might well be classified as Rococo. As these two composers matured, their music took on significant changes that place them in the category now known as Classic.

In 1761, Haydn, then aged twenty-nine, went to work for the wealthy Esterhazy family in Hungary. His very first compositions for Prince Esterhazy were the three symphonies called "Morning," "Noon," and "Evening." These were designed to show the Prince what Haydn could do in the way of writing music to please not only the Prince but to entertain his guests. These little symphonies are exquisite examples of Haydn's early work.

In 1772, Mozart, then only sixteen, was employed by Archbishop Hieronymous von Colloredo of Salzburg, Austria. It was his duty, among other things, to compose music to entertain the Archbishop and his friends. For them, Mozart wrote a number of suites which he called "Serenades" and "Divertimenti." "Serenade" implies night music while "Divertimento" implies music as a pleasing diversion. These lighthearted, youthful works are indeed pleasant. Although never intended to be taken seriously, some of them remain in the permanent repertoire of chamber music because of their beauty and charm.

Rococo music is not profound—it was never intended to be— nor is it trivial in any sense of the word. It was written with the idea of being entertaining and it is indeed delightful. It has dignity and charm like the gallantry of the period. Much of it has a great deal of melodic ornamentation (such as trills) but this must not be thought of as superficial but as an essential part of the melody.

Although much Pre-Classic and Rococo music was written for entertainment, it is quite possible that as Mozart and Haydn matured and developed, the tastes of their patrons and audiences developed along with them. The listener also will find that his

53

taste for Classic music will develop as he listens to these compositions written in a lighter vein.

Rococo music for a few instruments or for chamber orchestra was intended for small audiences in intimate surroundings. This kind of music then adapts itself very favorably to recordings to be listened to under similar circumstances in your own home.

Since Rococo music is all easy listening, very little comment is made about many of the following suggested compositions. They are listed according to form to enable the listener to locate readily the music that may interest him.

Suggested Music for Various Solo Instruments:

Bach C. P. E.: "Piano Sonatas"
Couperin, François: *Messe a L'usage des Couvents* (organ)
> A sincerely inspirational suite of pieces for use in the Mass. This ranks among the finest of organ music by a French composer of the period.

Rameau: *Pièces de Clavecin* (harpsichord)
> Some of these are usually available in suite form.

Scarlatti, Domenico: "Sonatas for Harpsichord"
> The composer wrote nearly six hundred of these short charming pieces that are in one movement only.

Tartini: Sonata in g minor for Violin, "Devil's Trill"
> This is quite a favorite among violinists and the best-known work of the composer.

Suggested Music for a Few Instruments:

Bach, C. P. E.: *Drey Quartetten für Fortepiano, Flöte und Bratsche*
> As was customary, the violoncello was added to reinforce the bass—hence the title "Quartetten." In the composer's own handwriting we learn that this quartet was written for piano, flute, and viola. The piano should not be replaced by a harpsichord as is often done.

Bach, J. C.: "Quartet for Flute, Violin, Viola, and Cello"
Couperin, François: Concert *Les Goûts-Réunis*, No. 6 (suite of five pieces)
> The Concerts *Goûts-Réunis* were written as if they were to be played on a keyboard instrument. According to a note by the composer they were intended to be played by any "reasonable" combination of instruments. *"Air du Diable"*

in this suite is a favorite display piece for the flute which is traditionally given the solo part.

Couperin, François: Trio Sonata *"L'Astre"*
Written for Flute, Violin, and continuo (Cello and Harpsichord)

Couperin, François: Trio Sonata *"L'Impériale"*
Written for two Violins and continuo (Cello and Harpsichord)

Couperin, François: *La Steinquerque* (suite of five pieces)
Sometimes this is called Trio Sonata "Steinquerque." This is written for compatible instruments and sometimes augmented by adding more than those required for the average trio sonata. For example it may be played by violin, viola, cello, oboe, bassoon, and harpsichord.

Mozart: String Quartets, K. 80, K. 155, K. 156, K. 157
These four quartets are delightful. After hearing them you may be astonished to learn that they were written when Mozart was between the ages of fourteen and seventeen!

Suggested Music for Various Solo Instruments and Orchestra:

Boccherini: Concerto in B flat for Cello and Orchestra

Haydn: Concerti for Harpsichord in D Major, G Major, and F Major
These harpsichord concerti are Rococo art deluxe. Don't miss them.

Haydn: Concerto No. 1 for Organ and Orchestra in C Major
This concerto, dating from 1756, is the first of three organ concerti. The other two, dated 1763 and 1766, are in more Classic style and even tend toward the Romantic.

Telemann: Suite in a minor for Flute and Orchestra
This is a beautiful example of the many compositions of Telemann who was a very prolific composer. Although a German, Telemann took great delight in writing in the style of the French Rococo composers of his time.

Suggested Music for Chamber Orchestra:

Bach, C. P. E.: Symphony in D Major
This symphony for two flutes, two oboes, bassoon, two horns, strings, and continuo is probably the composer's best-known orchestral work.

Bach, Johann Christian: Sinfonia for Double Orchestra in E flat Major. Op. 18, No. 1
The conversation between the two small orchestras—reminis-

cent of the concerto grosso but in a lighter mood—is charming. The first and third movements are antiphonal and in a jolly mood. The second movement is slow and dainty.

Geminiani: Six Concerti Grossi, Op. 3 (published in 1733)
   Although in a Baroque form these concerti are in a very light, engaging, gallant style.

Haydn: Divertimento in E flat, "Echo"
   A delightful composition for stereo fans who enjoy one speaker "answering" the other.

Haydn: Symphony No. 6 in D Major, "Morning"

Haydn: Symphony No. 7 in C Major, "Noon"

Haydn: Symphony No. 8 in G Major, "Evening"
   These three symphonies should be in every library.

Mozart: Divertimento No. 2, K. 131 (1772—Mozart was sixteen years of age)
   Scored for woodwinds, four horns, and strings, this composition is in six movements and is cast in concerto grosso style. Each choir has its turn of importance.

Mozart: Divertimento No. 17, K. 334
   This suite of six movements is scored for string orchestra and two horns. The important part for the first violin makes this, in actuality, a suite for solo violin and chamber orchestra.

Mozart: "Serenade," K. 239, *Serenata Notturna* (1776)

Mozart: "Serenade," K. 250, "Haffner" (1776)

Mozart: "Serenade," K. 320, "Posthorn Serenade" (1779)
   These serenades are like suites in 3, 8, and 7 movements respectively. The first was written for a New Year's Eve celebration, the second for a wedding celebration, and the third with interest in the French hunting horn or posthorn (without valves), the predecessor of the contemporary French horn.

Rameau: *Six Concerts,* in six parts (Concerts en *sextuor*), (for six string instruments)
   These suites are pleasant, delightful, and easy listening. Most have programmatic titles. A few pieces are arrangements of some of Rameau's harpsichord music.

Suggested Vocal Music:

Gluck: *Orpheus and Euridice* (opera)
   One of the oldest operas in the repertoire today. Orpheus visits the underworld in search of his beloved Euridice.

This plot was a favorite among many composers and this opera should not be confused with others by the same name.

Rameau: *La Guirlande* (The Garland)

This is a pastoral ballet with vocal music. The plot is rather trivial but the music is beautiful. It is scored for soprano, tenor, chorus, and orchestra. Along with the ballet and the dances of the day, Rameau trots out all of the tricks of the trade. The result is a good theatrical production.

Rameau: Pygmalion *(Acte de Ballet*—"Opera-ballet")

The sculptor, Pygmalion, creates a statue of a lovely woman with which he falls in love. The statue comes to life. Pygmalion exclaims to the god of love, "Direct your arrows to our hearts." The original text by Houdart de La Motte called "La Sculpture" (1700) was revised by Ballot de Savot for Rameau. The Broadway hit, *My Fair Lady,* is a recent revival of the same plot considerably revised by way of *Pygmalion,* the play by George Bernard Shaw.

Scarlatti, Alessandro: *Su le Spone del Tebro* (a secular cantata)

For solo voice, strings, and trumpet, this fine and exciting composition has florid, lyric, and dramatic arias and recitatives with contrasting moods depicting conflicts in a love story. Time: twenty minutes.

Chapter Seven

CLASSIC
(1750-1825)

THE CLASSIC SYMPHONY ORCHESTRA

WE ARE INDEBTED to Franz Joseph Haydn (1732–1809) for organizing and establishing the nucleus of the present-day symphony orchestra. He discarded many ancient instruments and none of these ever appeared in the symphony orchestra again. The four choirs of the orchestra were firmly established. Orchestral music developed rapidly both in quantity and quality.

Wolfgang Amadeus Mozart (1756–1791) was one of the first to introduce the clarinet into the orchestra. Haydn approved of the instrument and later used it in his "London" and "Clock" symphonies. Although Mozart wrote for the harpsichord, the piano took its place in his major keyboard compositions.

Haydn and Mozart symphonies were written for some or all of the following instruments:

Strings	*Woodwinds*	*Brass*	*Percussion*
Violins	Flutes	Trumpets*	Timpani
Violas	Clarinets	Horns*	(Kettledrums)
Violoncellos	Oboes	(French Horns)	
Double basses	Bassoons		

The Classicists used the piano as a solo instrument and not as an orchestral instrument.

The trombone was used by Gluck (Pre-Classicist) in his opera *Alceste* and by Mozart in his operas *The Magic Flute* and

* Without valves until 1813. See page 71.

Don Giovanni but Ludwig van Beethoven (1770–1827) was the first to use it in a symphony.

These were the instruments that Beethoven used in his Symphonies Nos. 1, 2, 3, 4, 7, and 8. The orchestra was enlarged a little for his Fifth and Sixth Symphonies and greatly enlarged for his Symphony No. 9. Compare the above list of instruments with the list required by Beethoven for his Symphony No. 9, which is scored for chorus, solo voices, and these instruments:

Strings	*Woodwinds*	*Brass*	*Percussion*
1st Violins	1 Piccolo	2 Trumpets	2 Timpani
2nd Violins	2 Flutes	4 Horns	Triangle
Violas	2 Clarinets	3 Trombones	Cymbals
Violoncellos	2 Oboes		Bass Drum
Double basses	2 Bassoons		
	1 Contrabassoon		

CHARACTERISTICS OF MUSIC OF HAYDN, MOZART, AND BEETHOVEN

Haydn and Mozart presented the emotional in music with dignified reserve and charm; they approached climaxes with considerable restraint, and wrote melodies that are quite songlike and easy to listen to. Their orchestral compositions were written in clear, transparent style and in traditional forms that are easily comprehended. They wrote for sophisticated audiences, mostly for courts, and with a few exceptions, their instrumental music was absolute. Absolute music is music in which the composer presents various more or less indescribable moods that have no literary or pictorial association.

The characteristics of instrumental music of Haydn and Mozart may be more easily comprehended in outline form:

1. Emotion—reserved, in moderation
2. Melodies—songlike
3. Climaxes—reserved
4. Orchestration—transparent
5. Forms—clear, well-defined
6. Primarily absolute

The characteristics of the instrumental music of Haydn and Mozart may well apply to the instrumental music of Beethoven except in his later compositions (those written after 1800, which include all his symphonies except the first) there is much less restraint in emotional qualities. Beethoven's later period marks a transition from pure Classicism to Romanticism.

59

THE CLASSIC SYMPHONY

The classic sonata is a structural form for solo instrument such as the piano or violin; two instruments such as a sonata for violin and piano; and for groups of instruments also. A sonata for three instruments is called a "trio"—for four instruments, a "quartet"—for five instruments, a "quintet," etc. A classic symphony has the same general structural form.

The typical classic symphony is composed of four movements or independent sections, usually named by Italian tempo terms such as are listed on page 160. The general scheme of the four movements is as follows:

First movement (fast)—Contrasting themes but, in general, quite cheerful and spirited.

Second movement (slow)—Songlike, lyrical, melodic.

Third movement (medium fast)—Dancelike.

Fourth movement (fast)—Usually full of vitality, ending with a "lift."

ANALYSIS OF BEETHOVEN'S FIFTH SYMPHONY

This symphony has been chosen for analysis because it is generally accepted as a standard of form. Beethoven's Fifth Symphony would be programmed as follows:

Symphony No. 5 in c minor, Op. 67 . . . Beethoven

Allegro con brio
Andante con moto
Allegro
Allegro maestoso

Allegro Con Brio

The Sonata-Allegro form may have as many as five subdivisions. They are as follows: (1) Introduction; (2) Exposition—main themes are introduced; (3) Development—a sort of unfolding of thematic material; (4) Recapitulation—restatement of themes; (5) Coda—a sort of conclusion or "epilogue."

The introduction or the coda, or both, may be omitted. In this movement, the introduction is omitted. In the Sonata-Allegro form, as in all other forms, we find little changes here and there as in houses that fulfill the same general requirements.

There is a perfect union between form and content in the Sonata-Allegro form. Melodies appear and reappear in orderly fashion as logically and appropriately as the characters appear and reappear in a drama. As an aid to listening it is well to acquaint yourself with the first melodies or tunes that you hear. These melodies or tunes are going to reappear from time to time. They may reappear slightly altered, just as characters reappear in a play wearing different costumes.

The first movement is made up primarily of two themes called First Theme and Second Theme, or Principal Theme and Subordinate Theme. The very first four notes that you hear in Beethoven's Fifth Symphony make up the first theme. This theme is repeated immediately in a slightly lower position. Then in rapid succession you will hear it repeated over and over in still different pitches, seeming to tumble over itself. This "play of the theme" goes on for a while, then comes the transition, an "episode" leading into the second theme which appears to be slower and is quite different.

The following is an outline of the Sonata-Allegro form with discussions of the various parts of the first movement of Beethoven's Fifth. Notice how the composer develops a musical drama with symmetry and balance.

Sonata-Allegro form

I. Exposition (the main subjects are introduced)
    1. First Theme
    2. A Transition
    3. Second Theme
    4. Codetta (a semiending)—In this case it terminates with repetition marks which indicate that the entire exposition is to be repeated. This repetition, often called "recapitulation," is sometimes omitted, especially in records where time is to be considered.
II. Development (unfolding of the thematic material)
    1. Here the composer has a chance to exercise originality and artistry in the treatment of themes by modification, inversion, counterpoint, new combinations, changes in orchestration, etc.
    2. New and contrasting material is made up of a fragment of the introductory phrase that precedes the second theme in the Exposition. This is presented in a series of sequences and adds variety. Beethoven not only creates new interest in this way but also devises ways of returning to the first theme of the Recapitulation which follows.
III. Recapitulation or Reprise (restatement of themes)
    1. Restatement of the First Theme. Here Beethoven

places the theme in the bass against the full orchestra.
2. Note the very short unrelated oboe solo after the restatement of the first theme and brief reiterations of
it. This not only adds variety but new interest. If
we were to have exact repetitions of themes in this
section it would become very dull listening. As it is
there is always something that brings freshness.
3. The Second Theme transposed. Placing the second
theme in a new key helps give it a feeling of "new-
ness" since every key has a different tonal color.
IV. Coda (conclusion)
1. By the use of old or new material any composition
may be brought to a conclusion with a coda which
creates a final ending. In some cases it is a sort of
"epilogue" such as a concluding speech by an actor
at the end of a play.
2. Codas vary in length from very short to very long.
It depends on whether or not the composer wants
to drive home a point or have time to build up to a
climax or other dramatic effects.

Andante Con Moto

The second movement is in the form of theme and variations. A "Theme and Variations" is just about what the title
would indicate—a theme or tune first presented rather simply
and then changed in various ways as it appears from time to
time. It is not necessary to go into detail about the endless ways
that a theme may be varied. Think of variations as you would
a character in a play who, every time he appears, is in a different
frame of mind.

To follow the entire construction, refer to Work Sheet No.
2. The Principal Theme is in two parts. The very first tune that
you hear is Part I. It is slow, short, and songlike. It is followed
by two short phrases by the string choir, each of which is "echoed"
by the woodwind choir. Part II of the Principal Theme then
appears in the clarinets. In the Work Sheet II—1st period, and
II—2nd period the tune is approximately the same. Note that
sometimes the tune is very evident—somtimes it is a little obscure.

Allegro

The third movement is in Ternary form. It is made up of
two sections—"A" and "B." The pattern is A-B-A. This estab-

lishes a certain sense of balance. The first "A"—Principal Section (Outline below) is a Rondo, a-b-a-b-a.

The three terms Rondo, Rondo form, and Rondo-Sonata form mean the same thing. For the sake of convenience we shall refer to this form as the Rondo. With letters used to name the sections, as in the ternary form above, in the rondo we may have a construction such as a-b-a-b-a, a-b-a-c-a, or r-a-r-b-r-a-r. In the last, the "r" represents the "Rondo theme." There are many more possible patterns. The general idea is to give the composition balance and symmetry. These forms are frequently used in one or more movements of the classical sonatas, symphonies, and concertos.

In the following outline of the third movement of the Fifth Symphony, note the construction of the "A" or Principal Section. When broken down, we have a rondo—pattern a-b-a-b-a.

Listen to melodies as you follow the outline. The "a" theme is at the very beginning—played by the cellos and double basses—and is very short. The "B" section is called "Trio"— or middle section (not a composition for three instruments or voices). The construction here is a-a-b-a-b.

The "A" or Principal Section follows in Ternary Form with a Codetta leading into the Fourth Movement without pause. Note the lighter character of the themes played by the woodwinds, etc.

Outline, Third Movement, Beethoven's Fifth Symphony

A- - - Principal Section
    a - Part I - Principal Theme - 1st period
    b - Part I - Principal Theme - 2nd period
    a - Part II - Principal Theme - 1st period
    b - Part II - Principal Theme - 2nd period
    a - Part III - Principal Theme - 1st period
    Codetta - (a sort of semiending)
B- - - Trio
    a - Part I - 1st Theme
    a - Part I - 1st Theme
    b - Part II - 2nd Theme
    a - Part III - 1st Theme
    b - Part IV - 2nd Theme
    a - Part V - 1st Theme
    Transition
A- - - Principal Section
    a - Part I - Principal Theme - 1st period
    b - Part I - Principal Theme - 2nd period

a - Part II - Principal Theme - 1st period
    Codetta (a semiclose leading directly into the fourth
    movement)

Allegro Maestoso

The fourth movement is in Sonata-Allegro Form—same as
the first movement.

SYMPHONIES OF HAYDN, MOZART, AND BEETHOVEN

Suggested Mozart Symphonies:

Symphony No. 32 in G Major, K. 318 (1779)
Symphony No. 36 in C, K. 425, "Linz" (1783)
Symphony No. 38 in D Major, K. 504, "Prague" (1787)
Symphony No. 39 in E flat Major, K. 543 (1788)
Symphony No. 40 in g minor, K. 550 (1788)
Symphony No. 41 in C Major, K. 551, "Jupiter" (1788)

Suggested Haydn Symphonies:

Symphony No. 92, "Oxford" (1788)
Symphony No. 94, "Surprise" (1791)
Symphony No. 96, "The Miracle" (1791)
Symphony No. 100, "Military" (1794)
Symphony No. 101, "Clock" (1794)
Symphony No. 103, "Drum Roll" (1795)
Symphony No. 104, "London" (1795)

Suggested Beethoven Symphonies:

Symphony No. 3 in E flat, Op. 55, "Eroica" (1806)
Symphony No. 5 in c minor, Op. 67 (1807)
Symphony No. 6 in F, Op. 68, "Pastorale"
Symphony No. 7 in A, Op. 92 (completed in 1812)
    The "Pastorale" has programmatic content indicated by the
composer in the subtitles: "Cheerful impressions on arriving in
the country," "By the brook," "Peasants merrymaking," "The
storm," and "The shepherd's hymn."
    It is interesting to note that the Beethoven symphonic litera-
ture is more popular in America than that of any other composer. If you are a Beethoven fan do not hesitate to try any of
his nine symphonies.

THE CLASSIC SOLO CONCERTO

The Classic solo concerto in its typical form has three movements. The first movement is fast; the second, slow; the third, very fast. Near the end, or at the end of the first movement we can expect a cadenza.

A cadenza is a section played by the solo instrument. It varies in length. In the Classic concertos it is usually quite long, especially in the Beethoven concertos. It is in free style and is virtuoso in character. Here the solo artist has a chance to display his technical skill. The subject material is usually from themes of the movement, interspersed with new ideas. Many times it serves as a coda with a lot of "fireworks."

The Classic Piano Concerto

The piano is an excellent solo instrument with orchestra. Its timbre is so different from the orchestra; its power of dynamics so variable (from very soft to very loud) that it can give meaning to the daintiest passages of Mozart and the most thunderous and dramatic episodes of Beethoven. The piano concerto has always been popular since it was first introduced during the Classic period.

Mozart's piano concertos and Beethoven's piano Concerto No. 1 are to be recommended for those who are looking for refinement, grace, and Classic charm. Beethoven's Piano Concertos Nos. 3, 4, and 5 are quite Romantic and also dramatic.

Suggested Classic Piano Concertos:

Mozart: Concerto No. 20, K. 466
Mozart: Concerto No. 23, K. 488
Mozart: Concerto No. 27, K. 595
Beethoven: Concerto No. 1, Op. 15
Beethoven: Concerto No. 3, Op. 37
Beethoven: Concerto No. 4, Op. 58
Beethoven: Concerto No. 5, Op. 73, "Emperor"

The Classic Violin Concerto

The violin concertos of the Classic period are perhaps a little more restrained than the piano concertos. They lend themselves a little more to the intimacy that one expects of a string orchestra or a string quartet. Acquaint yourself with a Mozart violin concerto and enjoy the charm of this musical form.

Suggested Violin Concertos:

Mozart: Concerto No. 4, in D, K. 218
Mozart: Concerto No. 5, in A, K. 219
Beethoven: *Concerto for Violin and Orchestra*, Op. 61

Suggested Miscellaneous Concertos:

Beethoven: Concerto for Violin, Cello, Piano, and Orchestra, Op. 56
Haydn: Concerto in C for Cello and Orchestra
Haydn: Concerto in E flat for Trumpet and Orchestra
Mozart: *Sinfonia Concertante* in E flat Major for Violin, Viola, and Orchestra, K. 364.
Mozart: Concerto for Flute, Harp, and Orchestra, K. 299
Mozart: Concerto in E flat Major for Two Pianos and Orchestra, K. 365

CLASSIC CHAMBER MUSIC

Chamber music is just about what the name implies—music for a small group of instrumentalists, intended to be performed for small audiences, in rather intimate surroundings—not in a large concert hall.

Chamber music is dignified—never boisterous. It does not have the great masses of tone color that we expect of an orchestra but is about the most intimate and charming form of expression in all music literature.

The melodic lines are easy to follow and, for the most part, the forms are easily comprehended. The movements vary in tempo and character, giving the whole composition a sense of completeness—a little concert in itself. There is nothing more relaxing for the music lover than a bit of chamber music that he has become well acquainted with. Listening to records of chamber music in your own home adds to gracious living.

The compositions suggested below are for three, four, or five instruments. If you are not acquainted with chamber music or feel a little strange in this field of listening, we suggest trying Mozart's K. 478, listed below, or Beethoven's "Archduke" Trio. The piano adds a little variety for the beginner. Mozart's *Eine kleine Nachtmusik* must not be overlooked. It is played by either string quartet or string orchestra. It is a very delightful Serenade (K. 525), in the form of a classic sonata. This number has always been well liked by both performers and listeners.

66

Suggested Trios:

Beethoven: String Trio in G Major for Violin, Viola, and Cello, Op. 9, No. 1

Beethoven: Trio for Violin, Cello, and Piano, Op. 97, "Archduke"

Haydn: Trio in A flat Major for Violin, Cello, and Piano

Mozart: Trio in G Major for Violin, Cello, and Piano, K. 564

Suggested String Quartets:

Beethoven: String Quartets, Op. 18, Nos. 1 to 6

Beethoven: String Quartets, Op. 59, Nos. 1 to 3, "Rosoumovsky"

Haydn: String Quartets, Op. 76, Nos. 2 and 3

Haydn: String Quartets, Op. 77, Nos. 1 and 2

Mozart: String Quartet in G Major, K. 387

Mozart: String Quartet in d minor, K. 421

Mozart: String Quartet in A Major, K. 464

Mozart: String Quartet in C Major, K. 465

Suggested Miscellaneous Quartets:

Beethoven: Quartet in E flat Major for Piano and Strings, Op. 16 (arranged from his Wind Quintet, op. 16, see page 140)

Beethoven: Quartet No. 1 in E flat Major for Piano and Strings
This is the first of three piano quartets to which Sir George Grove assigned Op. 152. It was written in 1785 when Beethoven was only fifteen years old. It was the first in this form by any composer. Mozart's first piano quartet was written a little later the same year. Beethoven was in Bonn and Mozart was in Vienna. Each thought that he was the first to write a piano quartet.

Mozart: Quartet in F Major for Oboe and Strings, K. 370

Mozart: Quartet in g minor for Piano and Strings, K. 478

Suggested Quintets:

Mozart: Quintet in A Major for Clarinet, two Violins, Viola, and Cello, K. 581

Mozart: Quintet in g minor for two Violins, two Violas, and Cello, K. 516

SONATAS

Suggested Sonatas:

Beethoven: Piano Sonata, Op. 13, "Pathétique"

Beethoven: Piano Sonata, Op. 27, No. 2, "Moonlight"

Beethoven: Piano Sonata, Op. 57, "Appassionata"
Beethoven: Piano Sonata, Op. 110
Beethoven: Violin and Piano Sonata, Op. 24, "Spring"
Beethoven: Violin and Piano Sonata, Op. 47, "Kreutzer"

OVERTURES

For a discussion of the Overture see page 76.

Suggested Classic Overtures:

Beethoven: *Coriolanus, Egmont,* and Leonore No. 3.
Mozart: *The Magic Flute, Così fan tutte, Marriage of Figaro, Don Giovanni,* and *The Abduction from the Seraglio*

MASSES

Some of the best vocal music of the Classic period can be found in the Masses of Beethoven, Haydn, and Mozart. There is a wide range of expression and various musical interpretations of the Mass. The suggested list of Masses has been selected to include not only some of the best but also to include a variety. These Masses are all for solo voices—soprano, alto, tenor, and bass (except Mozart's K. 427 which is for two sopranos, tenor, and bass)—chorus, and orchestra. Haydn's include the pipe organ.

Suggested Masses:

Beethoven: Mass in C Major, Op. 86
Beethoven: *Missa Solemnis,* Op. 123
    The Beethoven Mass in C Major is much shorter than his more mature *Missa Solemnis* which is often referred to as the greatest of the period. They are both more Romantic than Classic in character. The *Kyrie* in the Mass in C Major is a high spot in this Mass. The C Major Mass is not as profound a work as the *Solemnis* but is a fine one for the person who is interested in a shorter Mass.
Haydn: Mass No. 4 in G Major (*Missa St. Nicolai*) (1772)
Haydn: Mass No. 7, *Missa in Tempore Belli (Paukenmesse)* (1796)
Haydn: Mass No. 9, *Missa Solemnis* (Nelson Mass) (1798)
Haydn: Mass No. 10, *Missa Solemnis (Theresienmesse)* (1799)
    Haydn's earliest Mass listed here was written for Prince Nicholas Esterhazy. It is quite pastoral and lyrical; imbued with the Christmas spirit; and it is often called the "Christmas Mass." Haydn's last six Masses, three of which are suggested here, are much more dramatic and operatic in charac-

ter. These later Masses are on a large scale and reflect Haydn's increasing interest in the orchestra. Number 7, Mass in Time of War, is at times quiet and devotional. However, for the most part, it leaves the listener with a feeling of anxiety, unrest, and a militaristic spirit. The use of the timpani throughout the Mass is effective, especially in the *Agnus Dei*, hence this Mass is referred to as the *Paukenmesse* (Drum Mass). Number 9 is very festive, dramatic, and operatic in character. It was composed in honor of Prince Esterhazy's distinguished visitor, Lord Nelson, hence it is known as "Nelson Mass." Mass No. 10 is known as *Theresienmesse,* presumably alluding to Marie Therese, second wife of Emperor Francis II. Like Nos. 7 and 9 it ranges in mood from the devotional to the festive and operatic.

Mozart: Mass in C Major, K. 317, "Coronation"
Mozart: Mass in c minor, K. 427, "The Great"

The Coronation Mass is sincerely devotional and more religious in character than the Mass in c minor which is operatic in character. The latter was written in a spirit of jubilation upon the recovery of Mozart's beloved fiancée, Konstanze Weber. Mozart did not finish the Gloria of K. 427 but from his sketches later editors have completed it. It may also be noted here that he did not compose an *Agnus Dei* for this Mass nor did he leave any sketches of one. Some editors have included an *Agnus Dei* which they made up from materials from other portions of the Mass.

Suggested Miscellaneous Vocal Works:

Beethoven: Symphony No. 9 in d, Op. 125, "Choral"
Haydn: *Creation* (oratorio)
Haydn: *Seasons* (oratorio)
Haydn: *Te Deum*
Mozart: *Don Giovanni* (opera)
Mozart: *The Magic Flute* (opera)
Mozart: *Marriage of Figaro* (opera)

Chapter Eight

ROMANTIC
(1800-1900)

CHARACTERISTICS OF ROMANTIC MUSIC

THE CLASSICISTS were restrained and conventional, emphasizing formal clarity in style and exercising moderation in emotion. The Romanticists of the nineteenth century were quite different. They emphasized the emotional and subjective possibilities of music and presented these qualities in a very accessible manner, appealing to the public concert audiences. It may be noted here that the first public concerts were held in London in 1672 and were well established in the larger cities in most of Europe at the beginning of the nineteenth century.

The general social revolution of the nineteenth century affected music as well as all of the other arts. Music became a part of the general cultural life of the people and the serious composers were thinking in terms of music for the general public. The revolt against tradition and classicism resulted in more freedom of expression.

Composers leaned toward program music, music in which they wished to portray or present some literary or pictorial idea through their music. Realism, effects that sound like something real such as wind, storm, waterfall, etc., became a type of expression in program music. Melodies became more emotionally expressive, climaxes were unrestrained and many composers paid less attention to traditional form.

Added to all of this "about face," we find a development of

nationalistic tendencies throughout Europe—a revolt against following the style of the Classicists. Music truly became an expression of certain social and national groups, and attracted the attention of people in all walks of life. Some very fine music was inspired by folk songs and folk dances.

With many improvements and additions to the symphony orchestra, and innovations in general harmonic treatment, composers created much greater tone color in orchestration than the Classicists who retained clarity and transparency in all their compositions.

The characteristics of Romantic instrumental music may be summed up as follows:

1. Emotional qualities—unrestrained
2. Melodies—more emotionally expressive than previously
3. Climaxes—unrestrained
4. Orchestration—greater tone color than previously
5. Form—less attention to tradition
6. An abundance of program music

NINETEENTH-CENTURY ORCHESTRAL DEVELOPMENTS

During the nineteenth century practically all instruments, except those in the violin family, were improved and new ones were added to the orchestra. The piano first appeared as a solo instrument during the Pre-Classic period. During the Romantic period and later it was used occasionally in the orchestra.

The harp is an ancient instrument, dating from about 3000 B.C. in Mesopotamia. It was used a little by Handel, Gluck, Mozart, and Beethoven, but was not included very often in the symphony orchestra until it was used by Berlioz, Liszt, and Wagner. The present-day double action harp was first introduced in 1810. It is called double action because each pedal may be depressed two notches, adjusting the pitches of different strings.

Although the English horn was invented in 1760, it was not used until in 1767 when Gluck used it in his opera, *Alceste*. However, Gluck discarded it from the score later on. It appears in Rossini's *William Tell* dated 1829, and was first used in a symphony by Berlioz in his *Symphonie Fantastique* which is dated 1830.

The tuba family is a family of three very mellow-sounding bass brass instruments. They are the tenor (euphonium), bass, and double bass. The one normally used in a symphony orchestra is the bass which has a four octave range—the highest note being the F above middle C. The double-bass tuba is also called a bombardon. If the double bass is made in a circular shape for use in a marching band it is called a helicon.

The celesta is a four octave percussion instrument played from a keyboard like a piano. It was first introduced by Tchaikovsky in the "Dance of the Sugarplum Fairy," in *The Nutcracker Suite,* dated 1891.

The saxophone was invented in 1840. There are six members of the saxophone family ranging from a high soprano to the bass saxophone. Although not commonly found in the symphony orchestra it was employed by composers of orchestral music as early as 1844, later to be used by composers such as Saint-Saëns and Bizet and more recently by Richard Strauss, Hindemith, Milhaud, and Ravel.

During the nineteenth century the pipe organ appeared occasionally in a symphonic work. Most notable of these is Saint-Saëns' Symphony No. 3, generally known as the "Organ Symphony," composed in 1866. Ralph Vaughan Williams' Symphony," No. 7, "Sinfonia Antartica," first performed in 1953, is an outstanding recent composition in which the pipe organ has an exceedingly important part.

THE SYMPHONIC POEM

In the years prior to the Romantic period, a few orchestral compositions were written with some definite program in mind. Vivaldi's *Seasons,* a group of four Violin Concerti, representing the four seasons of the year, is one of the earliest. Other types of program music that follow, such as Beethoven's *Pastoral Symphony* and *Coriolanus Overture,* and Berlioz' *Symphonie Fantastique,* tell stories or present descriptive moods through music.

Franz Liszt is generally given credit for being the first to present the symphonic poem. A symphonic poem is an orchestral composition in free form, designed by the composer to present certain literary or pictorial ideas. In this new type of program music for symphony orchestra, Liszt wanted complete freedom—not only freedom of expression but absolutely no tie to any traditional form. As in all other music, there is a certain feeling of completeness in symphonic poems, but they all vary in content and structure.

In listening to a symphonic poem, you have a great chance to use your own imagination. The composer's program is only a guide; the rest is up to you. It is quite possible that no two listeners will have the same reaction or "see" the same things.

There are so many books with fantastic programs about music, and unlimited "reading between the lines," that it is well in every case to refer to the original program of the composer, if he had one. Many times a composer just gives a composition a title and leaves all the rest to the listener. If the composer did not write down in words what he wished to present in music, it might be just as well to use your own imagination, instead of some other program as a crutch.

LES PRÉLUDES BY FRANZ LISZT

The following is a free translation of Liszt's preface to his score of *Les Préludes*. It is a paraphrase on one of Alphonse de Lamartine's poems from *Meditations Poétiques*.

"What is any life but a series of preludes to that unknown song whose first notes are sounded by Death? Love is the enchanted dawn of every life, but none go through this life without storm and strife. And who, when the storm rolls away, does not resign himself to pastoral calm and its pleasant life? Yet when the trumpet sounds the call, he hastens to the post of danger, that he may once more find in action, full possession of all his power."

The general purpose in both the poem and the symphonic poem is to present the idea that life is a prelude to eternity. In life, which has love as a constant source of inspiration, we have four phases or periods through which we all seem to pass. In the preface to the score we note that (1) we are born of love, (2) we have periods of strife and anxiety, (3) we resign ourselves to fate and enjoy the pleasant things of life, and (4) yet, when called upon, we rise to our full stature to carry on the struggle.

Let us see how Liszt portrays these ideas through music. *Les Préludes* is one single, continuous composition, but is divided into four different moods, each representing a different phase of life. The introduction is marked "Andante" (rather slow)—the other sections are called "Andante Maestoso" (rather slow and majestic), "Allegro ma non troppo" (fast but not too fast), "Allegretto Pastorale" (not very fast—in rustic spirit), and "Allegro Marziale Animato" (fast with martial animation). The program is so very suggestive that these sections may well have programmatic subtitles characteristic of the various reflections. Subtitles are inserted in the following discussion.

Andante ("Introduction")

First we hear a faint sound from plucked strings—silence—again this same soft sound. The first three notes that you hear after this, are the three notes that make up the "germinal motif" from which the entire work grows.

Andante Maestoso ("Love")

After the introduction the "germinal motif," in a burst of joy and enthusiasm, is played by the trombones, cellos, and bassoons. Liszt adds to the motif to complete his main theme, which we may call the "love" theme. This theme is played by the strings and then by the French horn. Very soon a new version of the "love" theme is played by the French horn. For the sake of identifying it later let us call this the *second* "love" theme.

Allegro ma non troppo ("Human Aspiration")

This is ushered in with the theme in the bass, presented in a quiet, mysterious, and rather ominous manner by the cellos. We are soon in the midst of a surging turmoil. There is much unrest, activity, and agitation, which subsides in a few minutes and we hear again the "love" theme—this time played by the woodwinds and strings.

Allegretto Pastorale ("Nature")

A new theme is presented here and may be called the "Pastoral Theme." It is a very jolly tune, rather rustic in character. Part of the theme is first played by the horn, immediately a part of it is played by the oboe, and then in full by the clarinet. This is indeed a very happy and restful section. The second "love" theme from the Andante Maestoso reappears and is played along with the "pastoral" theme. This is a good example of counterpoint—two themes played simultaneously, each having specific significance. Listen to these two themes or melodies as you would look at the two pictures printed from a film with a double exposure.

Soon the tempo accelerates and there is a fanfare of brass announcing that something important is about to happen. It is the approaching last section which is called "Immortality."

Allegro Marziale Animato ("Immortality")

The "love" theme is heard in a very militant spirit played by the trumpets and horns, answered by the trombones. This glorious ending is a grand climax to this symphonic poem—a thrilling musical portrayal of victory through immortality.

Suggested Symphonic Poems:

Dukas: *Sorcerer's Apprentice*

Mussorgsky: *Night on Bald Mountain*
Saint-Saëns: *Danse Macabre,* Op. 40
Smetana: *The Moldau*
Tchaikovsky: *Romeo and Juliet*

Suggested Descriptive (Symphonic Poem) Suites:

Mussorgsky: *Pictures at an Exhibition* (orchestrated by Ravel). Gnomes, The Old Castle, Tuileries, Bydlo, Ballet of the Unhatched Chicks, Samuel Goldenberg and Schmuyle, The Market Place, Catacombs, The Hut on Fowl's Legs, The Great Gate of Kiev.

Rimsky-Korsakov: *Coq d'Or Suite* (from the opera, *Golden Cockerel*)
  1. Introduction: King Dodon in His Palace, 2. King Dodon on the Battlefield, 3. King Dodon and the Queen of Shemakha, 4. Bridal Procession and Lamentable Death of King Dodon.

Saint-Saëns: *Carnival of the Animals*
  1. Introduction and Royal March of the Lion, 2. Cocks and Hens, 3. Wild Asses, 4. Tortoises, 5. Elephants, 6. Kangaroos, 7. Aquarium, 8. Persons With Long Ears, 9. Cuckoo in the Deep Woods, 10. The Aviary, 11. Pianists, 12. Fossils, 13. The Swan, 14. Finale.

SYMPHONIES

Three very attractive Romantic, descriptive symphonies are listed below. These follow very closely the idea of the symphonic poem, except that the story is divided into movements. Some hold that these are not symphonies but are descriptive suites. The composer in each case has given us a definite program.

Suggested Program Symphonies:

Berlioz: *Symphonie Fantastique,* Op. 14—subtitled "An Episode in the Life of an Artist."
  There are five movements, each with a subtitle. The subtitles are: "Visions and Passions," "The Ball," "Scene in the Country," "March to the Gallows," and "Witches' Sabbath."

Goldmark: Rustic Wedding Symphony, Op. 26
  "Wedding March," "Bridal Song," "Serenade," and "In the Garden."

Liszt: *Faust Symphony* in three character pictures (after Goethe)
  1. Faust; 2. Gretchen; 3. Mephistopheles.

Romanticists, although less concerned with form than the Classicists, wrote most of their symphonies in the traditional four movements. The general character of each movement usually conforms to the general ideas as set forth by the Classicists. That is, the first and last movements are generally fast and spirited, the second movement slow and lyrical, and the third dancelike. The Romanticists were much more emotional, generally less reserved, and wrote with much greater orchestral tone color than the Classicists.

The composers have not given us a descriptive program in connection with any of the symphonies listed below. They are all classified as absolute music, music without pictorial or literary content.

Suggested Symphonies (absolute):

Bizet: Symphony No. 1 in C Major
Brahms: Symphony No. 1, Op. 68
Brahms: Symphony No. 3, Op. 90
Brahms: Symphony No. 4, Op. 98
Bruckner: Symphony No. 4, "Romantic"
Chausson: Symphony in B flat, Op. 20
Dvořák: Symphony No. 5, Op. 95, "New World"
Franck: Symphony in d minor
Mendelssohn: Symphony No. 4, Op. 90, "Italian"
Saint-Saëns: Symphony No. 3, Op. 78, "Organ Symphony"
Schubert: Symphony No. 8, "Unfinished"
Schubert: Symphony No. 9, "The Great"
Schumann: Symphony No. 1, Op. 38, "Spring"
Tchaikovsky: Symphony No. 4, Op. 36
Tchaikovsky: Symphony No. 5, Op. 64
Tchaikovsky: Symphony No. 6, Op. 74, *Pathétique*

THE OVERTURE

The overture, as an independent piece, did not become a part of the orchestral concert repertoire until during the Romantic period. Overtures of the Classic and Romantic composers appear quite frequently on symphony programs today and are a very acceptable addition to these concerts. Little need be said about how to listen to these because they are all very enjoyable without guidance. However, some general ideas may be helpful in knowing what to expect of different kinds of overtures.

There are three kinds of nineteenth-century overtures.

They are: 1. Operatic Overture—an orchestral introduction to an opera or similar work, 2. Incidental Overture—an orchestral preface to a play, and 3. Concert Overture—an independent concert piece for orchestra.

In a preface to the opera, *Alceste,* Christopher Willibald Gluck (1714–1787) noted: "My idea was that the overture ought to indicate the subject and prepare the spectators for the character of the opera they are about to see."

Composers, after Gluck, followed his example and incorporated in their operatic overtures some of the thematic material of the opera. These portions are most often the best or "hit" tunes of the show. Because of these "hit" tunes, many overtures are still popular in orchestral concerts, while the operas for which they were written are no longer performed.

As a whole, no matter what the Romantic overture, you can be pretty well assured of easy, pleasant listening. None of them are excessively long.

Suggested Romantic Operatic Overtures:

Glinka: *Russlan and Ludmilla*
Rossini: *William Tell, Italiana in Algeria, Il Signor Bruschino, Cinderella, The Thieving Magpie*
Wagner: *Flying Dutchman, Tannhäuser, Rienzi, Lohengrin*
Weber: *Euryanthe, Oberon, Frieschütz*

Suggested Romantic Incidental Overtures:

Mendelssohn: *Ruy Blas, A Midsummer Night's Dream*

Suggested Romantic Concert Overtures:

Berlioz: *Roman Carnival Overture,* Op. 9
Brahms: *Academic Festival Overture, Tragic Overture*
Elgar: *In the South* (descriptive of joys upon visiting Italy)
Mendelssohn: *Hebrides* (also known as *Fingal's Cave*)
Rimsky-Korsakov: *Russian Easter*
Tchaikovsky: *Solonnelle "1812"*

BALLET MUSIC

A ballet is an artistic theatrical dance performed by a group of dancers in appropriate costumes to the accompaniment of music. The production is usually done with fine staging, scenery, and lighting effects.

The ballet, as a part of a theatrical production, dates back to the early Greek theatre. Very little is known about the music in connection with the early dance. One of the influential people to take an interest in the dance and the ballet was Louis XIV of France (1643–1717). He fostered the dance and the ballet, primarily because he himself was a great dancer. He was quite largely responsible for introducing into the court many new dance types such as the minuet, gavotte, bourrée, passepied, and rigaudon.

Many outstanding composers incorporated these dance types in their suites which are for concert performance without ballet. Of notable importance are the suites of Bach which were written between the years 1717 and 1723 (see page 35).

There were many fine ballet dancers during the eighteenth century and many accounts of brillant performances but little of the music has come down to us. The first important ballet music, as far as the listener is concerned, dates from the latter part of the nineteenth century. Léo Delibes' music for *Coppelia* is the earliest example. This ballet was first performed in 1870.

The ballet, as a complete story, is an artistic union of a story and the dance, with considerable pantomime. Tchaikovsky's *Sleeping Beauty* and *Swan Lake* are excellent examples.

An opera may have a ballet as an interlude—not essentially a part of the plot. It may be rather loosely connected with the story, but primarily serves as a diversion from the singing. An example of this type is "Dance of the Hours" from the opera *La Gioconda* by Ponchielli.

Another type of ballet music is that which survives while the opera for which it was written is neglected. Exciting music that falls in this category is *Le Cid* ballet music by Massenet, written for his opera by the same name. This ballet suite is made up of celebrated dances of different provinces of Spain. If you like Spanish music don't overlook this one. The dances included are: Castillane, Andalouse, Argonaise, Aubade, Catalane, Marilene, and Navarraise.

Les Patineurs (The Skaters), which Constant Lambert arranged from excerpts of Meyerbeer's operas *The North Star* and *The Prophet,* is equally exciting. This was first produced at the Sadler's Wells Theatre, London, 1937.

Suggested Romantic Ballet Music:

Borodin: "Polovetsian Dances," from *Prince Igor* (with chorus)
Chopin: *Les Sylphides* (orchestrated piano pieces)
Delibes: *Coppelia*
Galzounov: *The Seasons*, Op. 67 (always popular)

Massenet: *Le Cid*

Meyerbeer-Lambert: *Les Patineurs*

Offenbach-Rosenthal: *Gaîté Parisienne* (arranged from several operas)

Ponchielli: "Dance of the Hours," from *La Gioconda*

Tchaikovsky: *The Nutcracker Suite,* Op. 71

Tchaikovsky: *Sleeping Beauty*

Tchaikovsky: *Swan Lake*

INCIDENTAL MUSIC

Incidental music is music written to be played before or during the action of a play and to assist in establishing, supporting, or intensifying the mood of the drama. The term "incidental" applies to all such music, whether it be for stage, screen, radio, or television.

This kind of music is not new with the Romantic period. The early Greek dramatists found it to be a very valuable part of their theatrical productions. An example of incidental music of the Classic period is Beethoven's music for Goethe's *Egmont.* The Romanticists were the first to write very much for the theatre that is worthy of a place in the concert repertoire.

The three kinds of incidental music are: that which precedes the show (incidental overture); that played during the action of the play (incidental); and music between the acts or scenes (entr'acte or intermezzo).

Some musicians hold that the overture and entr'acte or intermezzo are not incidental. They are placed in that category here because, after all, they do assist in establishing a mood before the production and between acts or scenes.

One of the best ways to enjoy incidental music is to associate it with that part of the production for which it was intended. However, much good music written for the theatre is able to survive on its own. The popular conception or use of some incidental music has caused it to grow completely away from the production for which it was intended. For example, at a wedding, few people think of the original idea back of Mendelssohn's "Wedding March," written for Shakespeare's fantastic comedy, *Midsummer Night's Dream.*

Suggested Incidental Music by Romantic Composers:

Bizet: L'Arlésienne Suites Nos. 1 and 2

Suite No. 1—Prelude, Minuet, Adagietto, Carillon

Suite No. 2—Pastorale, Intermezzo, Minuet, and Farandole

79

The numbers in this suite are taken from the twenty-seven pieces written for Alphonse Daudet's drama, *L'Arlésienne,* which was first produced in 1872.

Grieg: Peer Gynt Suites Nos. 1 and 2
> Suite No. 1—Morning, Ase's Death, Anitra's Dance, In the Hall of the Mountain King
> Suite No. 2—Ingrid's Lament, Arabian Dance, Return of Peer Gynt, Solveig's Song
> These pieces were written for Hendrik Ibsen's play *Peer Gynt,* first produced in 1876.

Mendelssohn: Midsummer Night's Dream, Op. 21 and Op. 61
> There are 12 pieces that Mendelssohn wrote for Shakespeare's *Midsummer Night's Dream,* first produced in 1843. The most frequently heard in concert are: Overture, Scherzo, Nocturne, Intermezzo, and Wedding March.

NATIONALISM IN MUSIC

Any sincere composer is influenced by his surroundings, his native countryside, and all that has gone before him for generations—folk music, native dances, and the general culture of his people. When a composer sets out, consciously or unconsciously, to emphasize these characteristics in his music, he may be described as a "nationalistic" composer.

To set out to describe in words the characteristics of music of the different countries would be impossible, or at least unsatisfactory. Some composers have written major compositions which we might term "nationalistic" or having "nationalistic" tendencies and yet the same composers may write with a more or less international aspect as well. These nationalistic tendencies prevailed throughout Europe during the Romantic period.

The following is a sampling of music of different countries chosen to illustrate nationalism. For the most part, each of these compositions is rather characteristic of the country that it represents. Most of them were written during the nineteenth century—a few were written a little later.

Suggested music from various countries chosen to illustrate nationalism:

> Austria—Strauss, Johann: "Waltzes"
> Bohemia—Dvořák: "Slovanic Dances"
> Bohemia—Smetana: *The Moldau*
> Finland—Sibelius: *Swan of Tuonela*
> Finland—Sibelius: *Finlandia*

Germany—Weber: "Overture" to *Der Freischütz*
Hungary—Kodály: "Intermezzo (czárdás)," from *Hary Janos Suite*
Norway—Grieg: Norwegian Dances, Op. 35
Spain—de Falla: "Nights in the Gardens of Spain"
Spain—Granados: "Intermezzo" from opera *Goyescas*

NATIONALISM IN RUSSIA

By western European standards, Russian music is astonishingly new. Russia's first important contact with western European music was during the reign of Catherine the Great (1762–1796), who dictated the policies of the court.

Catherine the Great was a Protestant Prussian princess. She wanted to surround herself with all the culture that she had enjoyed in the Prussian court. She brought in many musicians from western Europe, including her *kapellmeister*, Dominico Cimarosa, who later succeeded Salieri as *kapellmeister* in Vienna. Classicism was established in the Russian court and furthermore it was accepted—because Catherine was Empress!

Musical Classicism was so deeply rooted in the minds of the people of the Russian court that it was accepted as a standard of style for many years. Not until Michael Ivanovitch Glinka (1804–1857) presented his opera, *A Life for the Tsar,* in 1836, did the Russians realize that there was a tremendous possibility for developing their own national music. Glinka's opera was not like the music that Catherine had brought to them but was inspired by the people—their folk songs, dances, and way of life.

A group of composers, known as the "Russian Five," worked together, held to their national heritage, and formed a Russian national school. The "Five," Mily Balakirev (1837–1910), Nikolai Rimsky-Korsakov (1844–1908), Alexander Borodin (1833–1887), Modesté Mussorgsky (1839–1881) and César Cui (1835–1918) took upon themselves the responsibility for writing true Russian music.

For many centuries Russia was in contact with oriental culture. Impressions of long standing left their mark, especially in southern Russia, and the result was that in much of the music of the "Five" we hear exotic influences. Exoticism in music may be described as musical culture not characteristically European.

Note the oriental "flavor" in the following compositions by Russians:
Borodin: "Polovetsian Dances," from the opera *Prince Igor* (1869–1876)

Rimsky-Korsakov: *Scheherazade* (Arabian Nights) (1888)
Ippolitov-Ivanov: "In the Village," from *Caucasian Sketches* (1895)
Balakirev: *Islamey* (piano solo) (1869)
Cui: *Orientale*
Khachaturian: "Lullaby," from *Gayne Ballet*, Suite No. 1 (1942)

ROMANTIC CHAMBER MUSIC

Romantic chamber music tends to be much more emotionally expressive than Classic chamber music. Although the tone color is the same, the harmonic structure of the Romanticists gives their music a lusher character. In general, Romantic chamber music is very accessible.

For the listener who has had little or no experience with chamber music we recommend starting with compositions that include the piano. Listening to Romantic chamber music can be a most delightful and rewarding musical experience.

The piano quintet is usually for piano, two violins, viola, and cello. However, Schubert's "Trout" quintet is for piano, violin, viola, cello, and bass. The piano quartet is traditionally for piano, violin, viola, and cello; piano trio for piano, violin, and cello; string trio for violin, viola, and cello; string quartet for two violins, viola, and cello. Other chamber music for more than four string instruments, such as string quintets, sextets, etc., is made up of various combinations.

Suggested Romantic Chamber Music:

Brahms: String Quartets, Op. 51, Nos. 1 and 2
Brahms: Piano Quintet in f minor, Op. 34
Brahms: Piano Quartet No. 1 in g minor, Op. 25
Brahms: Piano Trios No. 1, in B, Op. 8, and No. 2 in C, Op. 87
Brahms: Sextets No. 1 in B flat, Op. 18, and No. 2 in G, Op. 36 (2 violins, 2 violas, 2 celli)
Dvořák: Piano Quintet in A, Op. 81
Dvořák: Piano Trio in e minor, Op. 90 ("Dumky")
Fauré: Piano Quartet No. 2 in g minor, Op. 45
Franck: Piano Quintet in f minor
Mendelssohn: Octet in E flat for Strings, Op. 20 (4 violins, 2 violas, 2 celli)
Schumann: Piano Quartet in E flat, Op. 47
Schumann: Piano Quintet in E flat, Op. 44

Schumann: Piano Trios No. 1 in d minor, Op. 63, and No. 3 in g minor, Op. 110
Schubert: String Quartet No. 14 in d minor ("Death and the Maiden")
Schubert: String Quintet in C, Op. 163 (2 violins, viola, and 2 celli)
Schubert: Piano Quintet, Op. 114 ("Trout")
Schubert: Piano Trio in B flat Op. 99

FAVORITE WORKS FOR SOLO VIOLIN AND ORCHESTRA

Brahms: Violin Concerto in D, Op. 77
Bruch: Concerto No. 1 in g minor, Op. 26
Chausson: *Poém* for Violin and Orchestra, Op. 25
Glazounov: Concerto in a minor, Op. 82
Lalo: *Symphonie Espagnole* for Violin and Orchestra
Mendelssohn: Violin Concerto in e minor, Op. 64
Paganini: Violin Concerto No. 1 in D, Op. 6
Saint-Saëns: Introduction and Rondo Capriccioso, Op. 28
Sarasate: *Zigeunerweisen*, Op. 20, No. 1
Tchaikovsky: Concerto in D for Violin, Op. 35
Vieuxtemps: Concerto No. 5 in a minor for Violin, Op. 37
Wieniawski: Concerto No. 2 in d minor, Op. 22

FAVORITE CONCERTOS FOR PIANO AND ORCHESTRA

Brahms: Piano Concerto No. 2 in B flat, Op. 83
Chopin: Piano Concerto in e minor, Op. 11
Chopin: Piano Concerto in f minor, Op. 21
Grieg: Piano Concerto in a minor, Op. 16
Liszt: Piano Concerto No. 1 in E flat
MacDowell: Piano Concerto No. 2 in d minor, Op. 23
Mendelssohn: Piano Concerto No. 1, Op. 25
Saint-Saëns: Piano Concerto No. 2, Op. 22
Schumann: Piano Concerto in a minor, Op. 54
Tchaikovsky: Piano Concerto No. 1 in b flat minor, Op. 23

MISCELLANEOUS PIANO SOLOS

Brahms: Waltzes, Rhapsodies, Intermezzi
Chopin: Études, Scherzi, Preludes, Nocturnes, Waltzes, Ballades, Fantasy in f minor
Chopin: Sonatas—b flat minor and b minor
Liszt: "Hungarian Rhapsodies"

Schubert: "Impromptus"
Schumann: Carnaval, Op. 9 (suite)
Schumann: Symphonic Études, Op. 13

MISCELLANEOUS ORGAN SOLOS

Brahms: Choral Preludes (11), Op. 122
Franck: "Three Chorales for Organ"
Franck: *Pièce Héroïque*
Franck: *Grande Pièce Symphonique*
Liszt: Prelude and Fugue in g minor on the name of Bach
Reger: "Fantasy and Fugue" on the Chorale "Wake, Awake, a Voice Is Calling"
Widor: "Symphonies for Organ"

THE ART SONG

The Art Song is a song of the highest artistic quality. The text is usually a very fine lyric poem supported by, or fused with, a sympathetic melody and accompaniment. It is one of the greatest contributions to Romantic vocal literature. The German Art Song is called *Lied*.

The *Lied* or Art Song has become a vocal form well-beloved by both artist and audience. This is no small wonder when we consider that these songs are products of such great poets as Goethe, Ruckert, and Heine, combined with melodies and accompaniments by such composers as Schubert, Wolf, Schumann, Franz, and Brahms.

The listener today seldom pays any attention to the name of the author of the words. In years past it was just the opposite. For example, in London, Henry Purcell's opera *King Arthur* (1691) was then known as an opera by John Dryden (author of the libretto) with music by Henry Purcell. In Vienna, exactly one hundred years later, the opera *Magic Flute* (1791) was announced as an opera by Emanuel Schikaneder with music by Wolfgang Amadeus Mozart. Today, few listeners give much thought to the name of the author of the libretto of any opera.

The successful listener takes both the words and the music into account when listening to Art Songs because it is a far more expressive medium than either the music or the words alone. Another point of view is that in listening to fine Art Songs you get acquainted not only with fine music but with fine poetry.

Listening to Art Songs

To get an adequate understanding of the Art Song—what to expect and what to listen for—let us analyze it by way of the seven elements and see how the text, melody, and accompaniment are related and interwoven. This will give you some specific information about the mechanics of the Art Song (see Glossary).

Rhythm

Recite any poem that you know. Notice that the poem falls into more or less regular rhythmic patterns with accents on important or key words or syllables. The meter or rhythm of the music must conform to the meter of the text so that important words will be emphasized when sung.

Melody

Generally the rise and fall of the melodic line conforms to the rise and fall of the emotional aspect of the text. For example, a composer does not have a soprano sing high notes just to show off but perhaps to help bring out or emphasize an important syllable, word, or phrase in the text. Note the pitch of the human voice as it changes with the change of emotion.

Harmony

The harmony in the accompaniment is sympathetic with the meaning and spirit of the text. There are chords that express various kinds of emotion such as sorrow or happiness.

Tempo

The tempo or speed of an Art Song is very important in projecting the general feeling of the lyric. A poem with a joyous, exciting text would require a faster speed than one of prayer or meditation.

Dynamics

The volume (loud or soft) conforms to the mood and drama of the text. A song about a football victory would certainly be louder than one about a little girl singing a lullaby to her dolls.

Color

The color or quality of tone in the human voice changes with different emotional experiences. You can recognize this in the speaking voice. In order to sing Art Songs well, the voice must be well trained so that the singer can go through the whole range of emotional expression without faltering. Those who sing Art Songs must be great actors through vocal interpretation without physical acting.

Form

The Art Song may have one of three forms. (1) It may be strophic—every verse has the same melody and accompaniment like a church hymn, (2) modified strophic—some verses vary from the pattern of the first verse, or (3) "through-composed," in which every verse is different.

The Erlking—Schubert

Listen to Schubert's *Erlking*, a setting of Goethe's poem by the same name. A father is carrying his dying son on horseback—followed and haunted by the Erlking, the spirit of death. The piano introduction at once gives us a feeling of uneasiness and haste. The repeated notes represent the galloping of the horse while the quickened melodic figure in the bass represents the ominous cunning of the Erlking keeping apace with the horse as it is urged onward into the night. The father is trying to comfort the child as he hurries, trying to reach home before it is too late.

There are four characters in this drama—narrator, father, son, and the Erlking. Notice how the quality of the voice of the singer changes from one character to another and how important the interpretation is in this short tragedy.

The following is a free translation of the entire poem. The characters in this song are given here to assist the listener.

The Erlking

Narrator Who rides so late through night and wind?
It is the father with his child;
He holds the boy in his arms,
He holds him tightly, he keeps him warm.

Father "My son, why do you hide your face in fear?"

Son "Father, can't you see the Erlking?
The Erlking with his crown and robe?"

Father "My son, that is only a streak of mist."

Erlking "Lovely child, come, go with me!
Such merry games I'll play with you;
Where many gay flowers bloom in the field,
My mother has many golden robes."

86

Son   "My father, my father, can't you hear
What the Erlking is whispering to me?"

Father   "Be calm, be calm, my child;
That is the wind moaning through the leaves."

Erlking "My fine boy, won't you go with me?
My daughters will take care of you;
My daughters will play in the evening
And they will sing and dance."

Son   "My father, my father, can't you see
The Erlking's daughters in that dark place?"

Father   "My son, my son, I see it quite clearly.
It is only the gray willow tree."

Erlking "I love you, your beauty arouses me;
If you come not willingly I shall use force."

Son   "My father, my father, he is taking me!
The Erlking has hurt me!"

Narrator The father shudders, he rides faster,
He holds the sobbing child to his bosom,
He reaches home full of fear and dread—
In his arms . . . the child was dead!

Suggested Art Songs:

   Brahms: *Mein Liebe ist Grün* (My Love Is Green), *Sapphische
Ode* (Sapphic Ode), *Wiegenlied* (Lullaby)
   Franz: *Widmung* (Dedication)
   Liszt: *Die Loreley* (The Lorelei), *Wanderer's Nachtlied*
(Wanderer's Night Song)
   Schubert: *Der Erlkönig* (The Erlking), *Der Doppelgänger*
(The Phantom Double), *Du bist die Ruh* (My Peace Thou
Art), *Gretchen am Spinnrad* (Gretchen at the Spinning-
wheel), *Wanderer's Nachtlied* (Wanderer's Night Song),
Hark, Hark, the Lark
   Schumann: *Widmung* (Dedication), *Die Lotosblume* (The
Lotus Flower), *Die Beinden Grenadiere* (The Two Gren-
adiers)

Tchaikovsky: *Nur wer die Sehnsucht kennt* (None but the
Lonely Heart)
Wagner: *Träume* (Dreams)
Wolf: *Kennst du das Land* (Knowest Thou the Land)

THE SONG CYCLE

A song cycle is a series of art songs having some psychological association with each other, the same general character or some general unifying thought that makes the entire collection an entity.

An understanding of and sympathetic feeling toward the text of a song cycle makes it become a living, stirring work of art. When listening to an art song or song cycle, let your imagination take over to the extent that you become a part of the experience being related or portrayed by the singer. Listen as if it were of direct concern to you.

Let us take, for example, "Four Serious Songs" by Brahms. He wrote this song cycle after he learned that his dear friend, Clara Schumann, was on her deathbed. He gave the songs to Clara's daughter Marie but never wanted to hear them. These songs with texts from the Scriptures were to be, as Brahms wrote, "a very personal offering to the memory of your beloved mother." To get the full impact of their meaning one should read the Scriptures from which they came. The reference for the first, "It befalleth both men and beasts" is Ecclesiastes 3: 19–22; the second, "I journey on my way," Ecclesiastes 4: 1–3; the third, "O death, how bitter thou art," Ecclesiasticus 41: 1 and 2 (The Apocrypha); the fourth, "Though I speak with the tongues of men and of angels," I Corinthians 13: 1–3, 12, and 13.

Suggested Song Cycles by Romantic Composers:

Berlioz: *Les Nuits d'Eté,* Op. 7 (Summer Nights)
Brahms: *Schöne Magelone* (Magelone Songs) (15 love songs)
Brahms: *Vier Ernste Gesange,* Op. 121 (Four Serious Songs)
Elgar: Sea Pictures, Op. 37
Mussorgsky: Songs and Dances of Death
Schubert: *Die Winterreise* (Winter Journey)
Schubert: *Die Schöne Muellerin,* Op. 25 (The Miller's Beautiful Daughter)
Schumann: *Dichterliebe* (Poet's Love)
Schumann: *Liederkreis* (Song Cycle)
Wolf: *Intalienisches Liederbuch* (46 love songs and songs of love)

MISCELLANEOUS ROMANTIC CHORAL MUSIC

We cannot overemphasize the importance of familiarity and its relation to the enjoyment of music. This is especially true of some of the longer vocal works listed here. All of the following compositions have characteristic Romantic emotional appeal befitting the text.

Berlioz: *L'Enfance du Christ* (The Childhood of Christ), Op. 25

This oratorio is for alto, tenor, baritone, and two bass soloists, chorus and orchestra. It is not the robust Berlioz speaking but rather an exquisitely humble approach to the sublime "Childhood of Christ." The music is dignified, gentle, and rather on a small scale compared to other works of the composer.

Berlioz: *Requiem, Grande Messe des Morts,* Op. 5

This Requiem is truly colossal and operatic. It is a powerful work scored for tenor soloist, chorus, and orchestra. Berlioz went all out in grand style to make the most of the subject of the Day of Judgment.

Brahms: *Liebeslieder Waltzes*

Although scored for a quartet—soprano, mezzo-soprano, tenor and baritone—this delightful work with piano accompaniment is sometimes sung by a chorus. A chorus is less buoyant and could be called unwieldy when compared with a quartet that can sing this group of eighteen waltzes in a very flexible way with a good German lilt.

Brahms: Alto Rhapsody, Op. 53—Contralto Solo, Male Chorus and Orchestra

The *Alto Rhapsody* is a deeply moving work. The text is taken from a portion of Goethe's somber yet exciting poem *Harzreise im Winter,* a story of Goethe's journey through the Hartz Mountains to visit a hermit who had sought refuge from his self-imposed withdrawal in correspondence with Goethe.

The text of the *Alto Rhapsody* is that portion of the poem which deals with loneliness and renunciation. Brahms wrote this magnificent work with emotional understanding—he too had a lonely life.

Brahms: German Requiem, Op. 45

This Requiem does not conform to the accepted pattern of the Mass for the dead. In the first place it is in German—not Latin. Brahms, it seems, wrote this either for Robert Schumann or for his own mother. He chose his own text from the Bible, making it a more or less personal farewell. Like the Beethoven

Missa Solemnis, it is suitable for concerts only—not a religious service. The work is for soprano, baritone, and chorus. The parts of this Requiem are as follows:

1. Blessed are they that mourn.
2. Behold, all flesh is as the grass.
3. Lord, Make me to know the measure of my days on earth.
4. How lovely is Thy dwelling place.
5. Ye now are sorrowful.
6. Here on earth have we no continuing place.
7. Blessed are the dead which die in the Lord.

Buckner: Mass in e minor

This Mass conforms to the traditonal pattern of the choral Mass established in the early Roman Catholic Church. The text is identical with the Renaissance Mass (see page 27), but it is written in the style of the Romanticists.

Cherubini: Requiem in d minor

This Requiem is rather unusual in that it is written for male chorus only with orchestral accompaniment. Emotionally it ranges from the tranquil and sublime to the dramatic; *Diesirae* expresses the terrors of the last judgment while in the *Agnus Dei* we hear a gentle prayer for peace.

Fauré: *Requiem*

This beautiful Requiem has a devotional approach. It is a sincere expression of faith—not the terrors of doomsday that we find in some others such as the *Requiem* by Verdi. It is scored for soprano, baritone, chorus, orchestra, and pipe organ.

Mendelssohn: *Elijah,* Op. 70 (Oratorio)

This oratorio contains some of Mendelssohn's finest vocal writing. It has always been popular and continues to hold the attention of audiences. The text is concerned with the important episodes in the life of the prophet Elijah. The score contains the following arias:

"If with all your hearts"
"Lord God of Abraham"
"Hear Ye, Israel!"
"O rest in the Lord"
"Then shall the righteous shine"

Schubert: Mass in A flat Major (D. 678)
Schubert: Mass in E flat Major (D. 950)

Both the Schubert Masses are for soprano, alto, tenor, and bass soloists, chorus, and orchestra. The first is sometimes referred to as Schubert's *Missa Solemnis.* They are both recognized as being among the finest musical offerings for the church written during the nineteenth century. They both express praise, joy, and confidence shifting from pastoral to dramatic, from light to dark, from tranquility to turmoil—always with restraint and devotion.

Verdi: Requiem Mass, "Manzoni"

This Requiem was composed in 1874 in memory of Alessandro Manzoni. It is one of the most thrilling and deeply moving religious Masses of the whole Romantic period, scored for soprano, alto, tenor and bass soloists, chorus, and orchestra and written in typical Verdi operatic style. It is a long concert Mass in sixteen different parts.

OPERA AND OPERETTA

It is well to acquaint yourself with the different kinds of musical shows and some of the terms used in connection with them. The following are defined in the Glossary and are listed here for your convenience: Opera, Opera Buffa, Opéra Bouffe, Singspiel, Opéra-comique, Comic Opera, Operetta, Musical Review, Ensemble, Aria, Recitative, Libretto, and Leitmotif.

Preparing To Hear an Opera

A thorough study of the opera takes more space than is practical here. However, a few hints to the listener might be appropriate. There is much to be said in favor of good preparation on the part of the audience.

First of all it is well to have a libretto or at least to know the story ahead of time. Sometimes cuts are made, especially in long operas. If you plan to follow the libretto during the performance, you should take one of the performance that you are going to hear.

Be well rested and well fed before attending an opera. This is very important. A sense of well-being means a great deal to you in adding to your pleasure and enjoyment of any musical production or concert of any kind. You are more liable to be "in the mood" for good music.

If you have never seen an opera, choose one that may be easy listening. Put off the Wagner operas for some time—they are the most difficult of all. The list of suggested operas is intended to help those who have heard very few operas or none at all. If you are interested in records, we suggest that you start with albums of excerpts or concert versions. These will give you the musical highlights and all the "favorites" of the show.

Opera and Operetta Compared

Opera	*Operetta*
1. Tragedy or comedy	1. Comedy
2. Recitatives—some spoken dialogue	2. Much more dialogue
3. Extravagant production— finest soloists, choruses, scenery, ballet, orchestra, costumes, conductors	3. Less lavish
4. Plots—fine literary, mythical, biblical, or historical	4. Plots—more related to the personal experiences of the general audience

In both cases, the instrumental and vocal music, the drama, acting, staging, design, costumes, etc., are in good theatrical style.

The following nineteenth-century operettas or light operas are popular perennial favorites:

Offenbach: *Orpheus in Hades* (1858)
Offenbach: *Tales of Hoffman* (1881)
Strauss, Johann: *Die Fledermaus* (1874)
Strauss, Johann: *The Gypsy Baron* (1885)

Suggested Operas and the Years in Which They Were First Produced:

Bizet: *Carmen* (1875)
Donizetti: *Don Pasquale* (1843)
Gounod: *Faust* (1859)
Leoncavallo: *Pagliacci* (1892)
Massenet: *Manon* (1884)
Mussorgsky: *Boris Godunov* (1874)
Puccini: *Madame Butterfly* (1904)
Puccini: *La Bohème* (1896)
Rossini: *Barber of Seville* (1816)
Smetana: *The Bartered Bride* (1866)
Verdi: *Aïda* (1871)
Verdi: *Falstaff* (1893)
Verdi: *La Traviata* (1875)
Verdi: *Otello* (1887)
Wagner: *The Flying Dutchman* (1842)
Wagner: *Die Meistersinger* (1868)
Wagner: *Tannhäuser* (1845)

Chapter Nine

IMPRESSIONISM
(1890-1925)

INFLUENCE OF PAINTERS AND POETS

IMPRESSIONISTIC composers were influenced and inspired by the Impressionistic painters. These painters, such as Claude Monet, Camile Pissaro, Edgar Degas, Auguste Renoir and Edouard Manet, preferred to express their reactions or capture a fleeting glance, rather than paint with photographic precision. To do this they painted with shimmering outlines, with very little detail, and they often painted one color over another instead of mixing colors. When you look at a picture painted in this manner, you get a feeling of a fleeting impression and your eyes "mix" the colors. In other words the Impressionists suggested rather than emphasized reality.

Impressionistic composers were also influenced and inspired by a literary movement called "symbolism." Symbolism deals with indefinite generalities, indirect references, subtleties, and illusions. Among the symbolists were Stéphane Mallarmé and Paul Verlaine. The symbolists showed their aversion to Romanticism by avoiding the emotional, pathetic, tragic, and great problems of life. They were concerned with lesser subjects, directed attention toward refinement and emphasized the esthetic.

CHARACTERISTICS OF IMPRESSIONISM IN MUSIC

Impressionism in music is a revolutionary movement against Romanticism. Like the poets, Impressionistic composers avoided

93

excessive emotion. Like the painters, they preferred vagueness and suggestion to realism. Like both the poets and painters, they wanted to leave much to the imagination.

The two French composers, Claude Debussy (1862–1918) and Maurice Ravel (1875–1937), are generally recognized as the main representatives of Impressionism in music. From an esthetic point of view their works are quite similar but upon close examination we find that all who may be classified as Impressionists, or were influenced by the movement, wrote in different styles.

As a young man, Debussy was fascinated with oriental music and continued to show interest in it for some time. This may account for his many zigzag melodies that show exotic influence. He favored the whole-tone scale while Ravel avoided it. Ravel's melodies are more definite while Debussy's are sometimes a little obscure with fragments of melody here and there. Debussy was antagonistic toward form, while Ravel was not. Ravel's orchestration is superior. He is recognized as being one of the best orchestrators of the twentieth century.

The American composer, Charles Tomlinson Griffes (1884–1920) was an Impressionist who, like Debussy, was attracted to the exotic, yet his style was a little modified with some Romanticism "showing through." Another who did not ape any of his fellow composers was the Englishman, Frederick Delius (1862–1934). He was an Impressionist who also had Romantic tendencies. His pieces are very sensitive, show considerable emotional restraint but stir the imagination.

Ottorino Respighi (1870–1936), an Italian, shows Impressionistic tendencies, but goes a step farther, writing in a more advanced twentieth-century harmonic idiom in his development of orchestral tone color, which ranges from quiet, sensitive moods to the most vigorous dissonances.

Debussy, Ravel, Griffes, Delius, and Respighi had a few things in common. They all avoided academic developments in music. Not one of them wrote a symphony! They avoided pathos, tragedy, and emotional emphasis. Note the titles in the suggested list of music. The compositions listed are of a poetic and imaginative character, dealing with fleeting impressions, orchestral tone colors and moods ranging from the calmest to the most turbulent—from the most refined to the most boisterous.

Impressionism became an influence rather than a crusade. There are composers who, from time to time, have written some things in an Impressionistic vein. This would not identify them as wholehearted or full-fledged Impressionists but would rather testify to the universality of the influence of the movement.

Impressionistic music may be characterized by some or all of the following:

1. Vagueness
2. Elusiveness
3. Atmosphere
4. Successions of orchestral tone colors
5. Avoidance of excessive emotion

SOME TECHNICAL PHASES OF IMPRESSIONISM

The Scale—Active and Inactive Tones—Whole-tone Scales

A scale is a family of tones bearing a definite relation to each other. Let us take the scale of C major for example. On the piano this includes just the white keys starting with the first white key to the left of any of the two black keys. Counting this, which is named "C," as number one, play eight white keys to the right. This is the major scale of C. Within this family of tones we have active and inactive tones. Play the scale once more, but stop next to the top C. This tone is called the "leading" tone, because it is so active that it practically compels us to play C, which is called the "key note" (home base). The leading tone is the most active of all the tones in a major scale.

When a composer wants to come to a positive ending, chords with active tones are chosen to precede a definite close. When a state of suspense is desired, active tones are avoided. The whole-tone scale accomplishes this perfectly because in it there are no active tones. Start with any key on the piano and play a scale up or down the keyboard skipping every other key whether it be black or white—this is a whole-tone scale. The octave is then divided into six equal intervals. Listen to this scale and compare it with the major scale. Note how inactive it is. The whole-tone scale was a favorite with Debussy.

Color

Choose any white key on the piano—skip a white key and add the next white one—skip another white key and add the next white one. You now have a chord made up of three tones. Play any other key, white or black, within the octave (a range of eight white keys). Play different keys with your chord and note how the "color" changes. Adding an extra tone to a chord changes its color and is almost like painting one color over another to create fleeting impressions. Impressionistic music often has successions of colored chords.

Harmony and Melody

Classic and Romantic harmony emphasized contrary motion. Contrary motion is motion of one or more voice parts moving in the opposite direction of one or more other voice parts. For example if the soprano goes up, the bass moves down. Impressionists often had all voices moving in the same direction. This is called parallel motion if the voices are kept the same distance apart, otherwise it is called similar motion. A series of chords in parallel motion or similar motion in the whole-tone scale creates a feeling of vagueness.

Impressionistic melodies very often seem to avoid natural direction. Listen to a slow movement of a Classic or Romantic symphony. Note how easy it is to follow the melody and almost anticipate where it is going. Now play a number by an Impressionist and note how he creates a rather elusive melodic line by avoiding natural melodic contour.

LISTENING TECHNIQUES FOR IMPRESSIONISM

A composer is expected to have high artistic ideals and a certain amount of perfection in his work. Performing artists are expected to hold to the score and present it in an authentic, artistic fashion with great sensitivity. We, as listeners, must present ourselves in a receptive mood. Our mental attitude is a very important factor in our enjoyment or appreciation of music. This is especially true of Impressionism. Don't think or say, "This is not for me." Rid yourself of mental blocks.

The many different kinds of Impressionistic music provide music for every mood or frame of mind. Quiet, imaginative Impressionistic music with its vagueness is obviously not the type of music to listen to after an exciting football game. This would not be giving the music a fair chance. Choose some time when all is calm; when you are at peace with the world, and you want to do a little daydreaming.

Impressionistic music is perhaps the most imaginative of all. As a listener, you must use your imagination to a greater extent than with other types of music. The composer usually gives us a clue about the piece in the title but very few, if any, program notes. Impressionism is very elusive and personal. Very few react in the same way toward any one composition. There is so much that is indescribable with moods changing like clouds that have but fleeting moments of design and color.

We have all had the experience of watching clouds as they move slowly—change color—fade away. Listen to Debussy's

Clouds. His program note is but one sentence, *"Clouds* causes the appearance of the sky to change with the slow, solemn motion of the clouds, fading away into grey colors lightly tinged with white." The virtues of this piece are its vagueness, suspense, and atmosphere.

There is a great variety in Impressionistic music. All in Impressionism is not quiet and calm as in Debussy's *Clouds.* Listen to Respighi's "Pines of the Villa Borghese," the first one of the suite *Pines of Rome.* Respighi gives us a musical picture of children at play in a public park where the pines are old, tall, and stately. In the midst of ancient surroundings there is plenty of noise as we may well expect—loud clashes—excitement—all that goes with the experiences of normal children at play.

The three main things to remember about listening to Impressionistic music are: know the title or something about the piece; be receptive; give your imagination free reign. Sometimes a great deal of pleasure may be had by guessing what the name of the piece may be and what the composer had in mind. With some compositions it is quite possible to switch titles and make sense. It just means that you are looking at a subject from a different point of view. For instance the titles of Debussy's *Clouds* and *Festivals* could be exchanged. The clouds would become active as if before a storm and we would have a view of the festival after all of the celebrants had departed.

Suggested Impressionistic Music:

The titles of Impressionistic music are an important clue to the contents. For this reason all of the subtitles in the various suites are given in this list.

Orchestral Compositions

Debussy: *Iberia* (the Roman name for the Spanish peninsula)
  1. *Par les Rues et par les chemins* (In the Streets and Paths)
  2. *Les Parfums de la nuit* (The Perfumes of the Night)
  3. *Le Matin d'un jour de fête* (The Morning of Fête Day)
Debussy: *La Mer* (The Sea), Three Orchestral Sketches
  1. From Dawn to Noon at Sea
  2. Frolic of the Waves
  3. Dialogue Between the Wind and the Sea
Debussy: *Nocturnes*
  1. *Nuages* (Clouds)
  2. *Fêtes* (Festivals)
  3. *Sirènes* (Sirens) (with women's voices)

Debussy: *Prélude á l'Après-midi d'un faune* (Prelude to the Afternoon of a Faun)

Debussy: *Printemps* (Springtime—suite in two parts)

Delius: *Florida Suite*
  1. Daybreak
  2. By the River
  3. Sunset
  4. At Night

Delius: *Over the Hills and Far Away*

Delius: *Summer Night on the River*

Delius: *On Hearing the First Cuckoo in Spring*

Griffes: *White Peacock* (originally for piano)

Griffes: *Clouds* (originally for piano)

Griffes: *The Pleasure-Dome of Kubla Khan*

Ravel: *Rapsodie Espagnole*
  1. *Prélude*
  2. *Malagueña*
  3. *Habañera*
  4. *Feria*

Ravel: *Daphnis and Chloé,* Ballet Suite No. 2
  1. Daybreak
  2. Pantomime
  3. General Dance

Respighi: *Fountains of Rome*
  1. The Fountain of the Valle Giulia at Dawn
  2. The Triton Fountain at Morn
  3. The Fountain of Trevi at Midday
  4. The Villa Medici Fountain at Sunset

Respighi: *The Pines of Rome*
  1. The Pines of the Villa Borghese
  2. The Pines Near a Catacomb
  3. The Pines of the Janiculum
  4. The Pines of the Appian Way

Piano Music

Debussy: Piano Pieces—
  Clair de lune (Moonlight)
  Reflets dans l'eau (Reflections on the Water)
  L'Isle Joyeuse (Isle of Joy)
  Jardins sous la pluis (Gardens in the Rain)
  Préludes
  Poissons d'or (Goldfish)

Ravel: *Gaspard de la Nuit*
1. *Ondine* (Water Sprite)
2. *Le Gibet* (Gallows)
3. *Scarbo* (Nocturnal Imp)

Ravel: Piano Concerto in G Major
Ravel: Piano Concerto for the Left Hand
Ravel: *La Valse*

Miscellaneous

Debussy: *La Damoiselle élue* (Blessed Damsel) (Cantata for soprano, mezzo-soprano, women's chorus, and orchestra)
Debussy: *Danse Sacrée et Danse Profane* (Sacred Dance and Secular Dance) (for harp and string quartet)
Ravel: "Introduction and Allegro" (flute, clarinet, harp, and string quartet)
Ravel: *Tzigane* (violin solo with orchestra)

Chapter Ten

POST-ROMANTICISM
(1890-1945)

POST-ROMANTIC COMPOSERS

POST-ROMANTIC COMPOSERS were inclined to use larger orchestras, write longer symphonic compositions, and place greater emphasis on emotional qualities than any other group of composers in the very late nineteenth century and on into the twentieth century. They developed greater orchestral tone colors and used more advanced twentieth-century harmonic idioms than the earlier Romanticists. (An idiom in music may be rather loosely defined as being a "language" or style of writing.)

These composers should not be confused with composers of the twentieth century who have Romantic tendencies in some of their compositions. The emotionally expressive qualities are never abandoned but are present to some degree in all music. No art survives on a purely intellectual basis.

Among those who may be classified as Post-Romantic composers are: Gustav Mahler, Richard Strauss, Jean Sibelius, and Sergei Rachmaninoff. They carried the banner of Romanticism from the late nineteenth century into the twentieth century.

Gustav Mahler (1860–1911)

Gustav Mahler composed with profoundly deep emotional sincerity. He expanded the orchestra to enormous proportions and, in four of his ten symphonies (Nos. 2, 3, 4, and 8), he added vocal parts. He felt the need of words to help bear his musical message. His music was his mission in life—to him a tremendous responsibility. The texts that he chose seem so personal because they fit in with the philosophy of the man—one who was known for his constant anxiety about eternity.

Mahler's Second Symphony, *Resurrection,* is scored for an enormous orchestra, pipe organ, soprano and alto soloists, and mixed chorus. The fourth movement, "Eternal Light," is an alto solo. The fifth movement, "Resurrection," is about thirty minutes long but so varied with soprano and alto solos and duets, male chorus, mixed chorus and orchestra that no one need be alarmed about the length. The entire symphony takes about one hour and fifteen minutes.

We suggest that you do not listen to the entire work at first. Start with the fourth movement. Become well acquainted with this then get acquainted with the fifth movement. After you have put these two movements together, you will have your curiosity aroused about the first part of the symphony, and will be much more receptive to it. Your mental attitude is important—listen as if "you were there."

An acquaintance with Mahler's *Resurrection* symphony can be very helpful to those who have difficulty understanding the more difficult moderns. The emotional values in the vocal parts are more easily related to our own experiences. Between passages or sections that are easy listening are passages that are in more advanced melodic and harmonic idioms, or more in keeping with what one might expect of contemporary writing. You will be getting some advanced contemporary idioms in small doses and relief in the romantic idioms.

Mahler's *Das Lied von der Erde* is one of the greatest song cycles ever written. It requires considerable study and listening for the average person but anyone will be greatly rewarded for the effort. Both this and the *Resurrection* symphony are marvelous pieces to bridge the gap between Romantic and some contemporary trends. Mahler's idioms in his symphonies and song cycles are a combination of the past and the present.

For further listening suggestions for this symphony and the suggested song cycles of Mahler, see listening techniques for the art song and song cycle, page 84 and page 88.

Richard Strauss (1864–1949)

The music of Richard Strauss is full of poignant emotional expression. The dissonances, once shocking, are now accepted as a natural means of expression. Only the most successful, popular favorites are in the suggested list.

The two symphonic poems, *Death and Transfiguration* and *A Hero's Life,* are not only among the composer's most successful and best works; but are rather accessible listening. A listener must constantly increase his capacity to listen to longer works. These two are excellent ones with which to increase one's capacity to "stay" with the music because they are imaginative, full of interesting subject matter, and are psychologically well constructed. See Symphonic Poem, page 72.

The *Burlesque* for piano solo and orchestra, written when the composer was twenty-one, is growing in popularity. This brilliant work is full of lively, sparkling, happy music. Don't miss it.

The opera, *Der Rosenkavalier,* is a very popular and successful one. It is by far the easiest listening of all the Strauss operas.

Jean Sibelius (1865–1957)

The Finnish nationalist composer, Jean Sibelius, has been loved the world over for his *Finlandia,* an expression of patriotic fervor unequaled in all symphonic literature. His music is Scandinavian, very different from the other three Post-Romanticists mentioned. Sibelius' symphonic literature is quite varied—brooding, mystical, spiritual, patriotic, folklike, plaintive, robust—the full gamut of the emotions are to be found in his music with its appealing Nordic flavor.

Sibelius has been a patriot of the first order—loving his native Finland with its steeply rolling countryside, its forests, and its lakes. The patriot is heard in *Finlandia*—the north country and its legends are reflected in *The Swan of Tuonela.* These are excellent prerequisites for Sibelius' symphonies. The Second Symphony is a good one to start with.

Sergei Rachmaninoff (1873–1943)

For a time in America, the compositions of the Russian composer, Sergei Rachmaninoff, were among the most popular of all that may be classified as Post-Romantic. As time goes on, most of them are falling by the wayside. However, the four mentioned in the suggested list on page 103 seem to be holding their own with audiences and still appear on programs.

They are perhaps the easiest listening of all listed here under Post-Romantic. They are full of lush harmonies and emotional melodies that are easy to follow. Whatever Rachmaninoff has to say in his music, he says with enthusiasm. The faster movements are exuberant and at times irresistible. For those who want music for sheer pleasure, and music that is more enduring than the type that is written just for fun, we recommend Rachmaninoff's.

Suggested Post-Romantic Music:

Symphonies—
Mahler: Symphony No. 1 in D, "Titan"
Mahler: Symphony No. 2 in c minor, "Resurrection"
Mahler: Symphony No. 8, "Symphony of a Thousand"
Rachmaninoff: Symphony No. 2, Op. 27
Sibelius: Symphony No. 2 in D, Op. 43
Sibelius: Symphony No. 4, Op. 63
Sibelius: Symphony No. 5, Op. 82

Symphonic Poems—
Rachmaninoff: *The Isle of the Dead*
Sibelius: Finlandia, Op. 26, No. 7
Sibelius: *Swan of Tuonela*
Strauss: *Also sprach Zarathustra,* Op. 30
Strauss: *Ein Heldenleben* (A Hero's Life), Op. 40
Strauss: Till Eulenspiegel's Merry Pranks, Op. 28
Strauss: *Tod und Verklärung* (Death and Transfiguration), Op. 24

Solo Instruments with Orchestra—
Rachmaninoff: Rhapsody on a Theme of Paganini for Piano and Orchestra, Op. 43
Rachmaninoff: Concerto No. 2 for Piano and Orchestra, Op. 18
Sibelius: Concerto in d minor for Violin and Orchestra, Op. 47
Strauss: Burlesque in d minor for Piano and Orchestra

Opera—
Strauss: *Der Rosenkavalier*

Art Songs—(words by Friedrich Ruckert)
Mahler: *Ich bin der Welt abhanden gekommen* (I Am Lost to the World)
Mahler: *Ich atmet einen linden Duft* (I Breath a Gentle Scent)
Mahler: *Um Mitternacht* (At Midnight)

Song Cycles—
Mahler: *Kindertotenlieder* (words by Friedrich Ruckert)
1. Once more the sun would gild the morn
2. Ah, Now I know why oft I caught you gazing
3. When my mother dear

4. I think oft they've only gone abroad
5. In such a tempest

Mahler: *Das Lied von der Erde* (The Song of the Earth)
    (Eighth-century Chinese texts)
1. The Drinking Song of Earthly Woe (tenor solo)
2. The Lonely One in Autumn (contralto solo)
3. Of Youth (tenor solo)
4. Of Beauty (contralto solo)
5. The Drunken One in Spring (tenor solo)
6. (a) Awaiting a Friend (contralto solo)
    (b) The Farewell of a Friend (contralto solo)

Chapter Eleven

EXPRESSIONISM
(1910-1950)

INFLUENCE OF PAINTERS

THE TERM EXPRESSIONISM came into being in the early part
of the twentieth century and was used to denote a school of painters who were violent extremists; who dealt with certain radical
trends. Expressionists often dealt with the morbid. Their subjects were often distorted and in many cases shocking. Geometric
patterns and design took a prominent place in the new movement. This geometric approach came to be known as "cubism"—
a type of Expressionism.

Words cannot take the place of the paintings themselves.
The following list of artists and their works is recommended for
study: Pablo Picasso—"Three Musicians," "Nude" (charcoal
drawing), and "Sylvette" (Portrait of Mlle. D.); Vasily Kandin-
sky—"Improvisation No. 30"; Marc Chagall—"I and the Village"
(cubism); Marcel Duchamp—"Nude Descending a Staircase, No.
2" (abstraction); Salvadore Dali—"The Persistence of Memory,"
and "Inventions of the Monsters"; Yves Tanguy—"Rapidity of
Sleep" (fantasy); Joan Miró—"Personages With Stars" (fantasy);
Paul Klee—"Ventriloquist" (cubism); Fernand Leger—"The City"
(ideal example of cubism).

In certain aspects, expressionistic music is analogous to expressionistic painting. The leading figures in the school of Expressionism were Arnold Schönberg (1874–1951), Alban Berg
(1885–1935) and Anton Webern (1883–1945).

Expressionistic music is not for the average listener. It is the most difficult of all listening. But even though you may not care for it, a knowledge of some of the phases of this development will aid in understanding many other contemporary compositions that have traces of Expressionism.

Only musicians and the most rugged explorers are sturdy enough to listen to very much Expressionism. It has been quite aptly defined as "cerebral" music. If you are one of the rugged or curious, we hope that the following information and suggestions will be helpful.

Expressionism in music is a radical departure from all traditional standards. It is full of new experiences for those who have heard only the conventional. The melodic lines, with their odd and long skips, are not "natural," the harmonies are often clear uncushioned dissonances, and the rhythms are often complex and changing within the composition.

The term "Expressionism" is a very misleading one. In the arts it does not mean emotional expression but rather the personal expression of the composer—the inner self. If the prefix "im" in Impressionism means impressions of the outer world, the prefix "ex" in Expressionism indicates expression of the subconscious inner self of the composer.

ATONALITY OR PANTONALITY

Many creative artists forge ahead exploring new fields. Sometimes the composer finds new fields of expression within certain scales or families of tones, called "keys." When traditional keys do not serve his purpose he explores the possibilities of new ones. This is exactly what Schönberg did.

Let us review briefly what has happened to keys or families of tones through the centuries and the type of music that we associate with each development. Looking back, we think of each phase as being perfectly normal and acceptable, but when they were first presented or introduced, some of them were not accepted any more favorably than some of Schönberg's ideas are by many today.

Through the years the pitches within the octave have been changed and different order and arrangement of tones within the octave have been introduced. The Gregorian Chant was sung in an untempered or so-called "natural" scale; the church music of Palestrina was sung in a "mean-tone" system of tuning; and, although it may be traced back to 1518, the equal-tempered scale was not in practical use until during the Baroque period. The temperament (tuning) for Bach's *Well-tempered Clavier* (1722) was probably only approximate. During the Baroque period, major and minor keys were established as we know them today—a great preparation for Haydn and Mozart who explored refinement in the Classic style.

After the Classicists came the Romanticists who explored the emotional possibilities of the major and minor keys. It is interesting to note that present-day temperament of the scale was not adopted throughout all Germany until about 1800, the beginning of the Romantic period; and not in England and France until about 1850, the middle of the Romantic period.

In the latter part of the nineteenth century, the Impressionist Debussy revolted against emotional Romanticism. He explored the possibilities of the whole-tone scale and showed preference to it for purposes of vagueness and atmosphere. At that time Debussy's music was treated with scorn by many, but today we enjoy it and accept it wholeheartedly.

In the early part of the twentieth century, Schönberg explored the possibilities of yet another family of tones, or tonality. By using all twelve tones within the octave, he developed a new kind of music commonly called "atonal," which literally means "no key." From the composer's point of view, it is a "twelve-tone technique" or "method of composing with twelve tones." Schönberg refers to it as "pantonal." At the piano for instance, it merely means that you use all of the keys, both black and white, and one pitch is just as important as any other. This makes the music sound as though the composer had destroyed "home base" by avoiding points of resolution or repose that we find so frequently in earlier music. This is one reason for the strangeness in Expressionistic melodies.

SERIAL MUSIC

Schönberg devised a system whereby a composer uses all of the twelve pitches within the octave and arranges them in some arbitrary order and uses this established unalterable order of pitches as the basis and source of material for an entire composition. This pattern is called a "tone-row" or "series"—the composition is called "serial music." The rhythm or length of the notes may be changed, the various pitches in the sequence may appear an octave higher or lower than their original position, the series may be inverted or played backwards (retrograde) and the retrograde form may be altered as mentioned before or any altered form may be transposed to any pitch. A discussion of the many other possible changes and developments is too technical and not practical here. Composers will find endless possibilities with this system. Compare the above with the findings of the British Change Ringers. With twelve bells it is estimated that it would take thirty-seven years, three hundred and fifty-five days to play a total of nearly five hundred million different changes or patterns.

The unusual tonality, odd skips, and wild leaps in this type of music make it difficult to follow and remember. The listener must expect to hear any serial music many times in order to get acquainted with it.

POLYTONALITY

Expressionists sometimes composed with polytonality. This means that two or more tonalities are used simultaneously, like playing the piano with one hand in one key and the other hand in another key. The harmonic structure is usually rather thin so that all the melodic lines are clear.

MIXED RHYTHMS—POLYRHYTHM— DIFFICULT RHYTHMS

Expressionists, like many other contemporary composers, use many different rhythms in one composition. When these changes are rather frequent, the composition has mixed rhythms. Sometimes the rhythms change very rapidly from one to another.

Polyrhythm, the simultaneous use of two different rhythms, is also a common present-day practice. To illustrate polyrhythm, let us just suppose that in a single composition we have march rhythm and waltz rhythm going on at the same time. March rhythm, with four beats to a measure, and waltz rhythm, with three beats to a measure, played simultaneously, might be counted out and appear as in the pattern below. The accent or emphasis is placed on the first beat of each measure. Note that the common denominator "12" is illustrated by the vertical marks.

```
March  1 2 3 4 1 2 3 4 1 2 3 4 1 2 3 4 1
       |||||||||||||||||||||||||||||||||||||||||||||||||
Waltz  1  2  3  1  2  3  1  2  3  1  2  3  1
```

Some Expressionists and other contemporary composers use rather difficult rhythms. It is much easier to follow music if it has a "regular" beat. The average listener may or may not be aware of it, but if he can tap his foot to the music, physically or mentally, it seems to hold together better. Try tapping your foot to a waltz with accents at the beginning of each measure—ONE, two, three—ONE, two, three, etc. Now try a more difficult rhythm in the same way—five beats to a measure or seven beats to a measure. These are more difficult and certainly not as natural as the waltz with its three beats to a measure.

In brief, Expressionistic music has some or all of the following characteristics:

1. Atonality or Pantonality
2. Polytonality
3. Polyrhythm
4. Mixed Rhythms
5. Tone-row

LISTENING TECHNIQUES FOR EXPRESSIONISM

Expressionistic music in the twelve-tone technique is thought of as music for the intellect—more or less mathematical, without regard for human emotion. A composition intellectually conceived, full of complexities that are rather abstract, will, quite naturally, be baffling to the average listener. However, the author has found, in his classes of hundreds of students who know little about music, that many of the untrained listeners show keen interest in Expressionism.

When melodies are difficult to remember it delays enjoyment. You must give these melodies more attention, and remember that one or two hearings are just not enough! We have a great advantage in recordings, being able to hear them over and over again by ourselves or with someone who is interested in trying to "get" the music.

When one of Gustav Mahler's symphonies was performed for the first time, he conducted the entire work, then sat down in the audience while another conductor took over and repeated it. New compositions might have a better chance if this sort of thing were done more often.

Avoid absolute music at first—start with program music. You will probably be a little more receptive, trying to get the composer's point of view through his program. Remember that Expressionistic music is primarily the expression of the composer's subconscious self.

Schönberg's *Verklärte Nacht* (Transfigured Night) is not Expressionistic: it is very dramatic and emotional—definitely a Romantic composition. He wrote it in 1899 and arranged it for string orchestra in 1917. It was first used as the score for Anthony Tudor's ballet *Pillar of Fire* in 1942.

Schönberg's exploration of the atonal or twelve-tone technique started about 1907. His "Five Pieces for Orchestra," written in 1909, is a suite of program pieces. One of them, "Summer Morning by a Lake," shows traces of Impressionism. The dissonances in this suite are vigorous, meaningful, and not very difficult to comprehend. The melodic lines and the general atmosphere of the pieces are interesting and stimulating.

If, after listening to "Five Pieces for Orchestra," you are ready for more, we suggest trying Schönberg's concertos in the suggested list below.

Alban Berg was one of Schönberg's pupils. His *Violin Concerto,* one of the finest compositions written partially according to the twelve-tone system, is not easy listening for the beginner but is greatly rewarding to the sturdy individual who has patience enough to listen to the work several times.

Although Expressionistic music does not appear on programs as much as other types, every advanced listener owes it to himself to become well acquainted with a few selections. In our listening we need contrasts. A successful concert is very often arranged in chronological order to prepare the listener for the "moderns" at the end of the program. Why not arrange your evening of listening in the same way? You may be surprised at the pleasure you derive from this approach. The "moderns" will be more meaningful.

Suggested Expressionistic Music:

Orchestral—
  Schönberg: *Beleitungsmusik zu einer Lichtspielscene,* Op. 34 (1930)
    "Accompaniment to a cinematographic scene" is not intended to be in connection with any actual film but rather an imaginary one.
  Schönberg: Five Pieces for Orchestra, Op. 16 (1909)
    1. Premonitions, 2. Yesteryears, 3. Summer Morning by a Lake—colors, 4. Peripeteia (sudden reversal in dramatic action), 5. The Obbligato Recitative.
  Schönberg: *Verklärte Nacht* (1899)
    "Transfigured Night" is a symphonic sextet for string orchestra. As noted above, it is a very romantic symphonic poem—Wagner style—inspired by a poem by the same name by Richard Dehmel.
  Webern: Six Pieces for Orchestra, Op. 6 (1910)
    This is an interesting and unusual suite of unnamed pieces

in different moods. As Expressionistic music goes, it is rather accessible for absolute music.

Concerti (all difficult listening)—

Berg: Concerto for Violin and Orchestra (1935)

Berg was so grieved over the death and personal loss of a very dear friend that he seemed to want to create in this Concerto something to perpetuate her memory. The first of the two movements is a musical character sketch of the friend—the second depicts loss, sorrow, and transfiguration. He used parts of Bach's *"Es ist genug"* (It is enough), from Cantata No. 60, in the second movement, which is especially moving.

Schönberg: Concerto for Piano and Orchestra, Op. 42 (1943)

Schönberg: Concerto for Violin and Orchestra, Op. 36 (1936)

Vocal—

Berg: *Wozzek* (opera) (1914–1921) (experienced listeners only)

Schönberg: *Pierrot Lunaire,* Op. 21 (1912)

This is a series of twenty-one mood-pictures with text from Albert Giraud's cycle of poems which was published in 1884. It is sung in a style invented by Schönberg known as *"Sprechstimme"*—a vocal declamation in which the singer momentarily just touches upon the pitch indicated and then slides up or down. This technique is very effective in creating and bringing to life the moonstruck Pierrot—his secrets, his torments, his confiding in the moon, his temptations, and his loneliness. Every experienced and advanced listener should know this cycle.

Schönberg: *A Survivor From Warsaw* (1946–1947)

A narrator with orchestral accompaniment relates in English his terrifying experiences with Nazi cruelties. It is a tense, dramatic, and thought-provoking reminder of the past.

Chapter Twelve

OTHER
TWENTIETH-CENTURY MUSIC

WHAT IS MODERN MUSIC?

THE AVERAGE person seems to think that compositions with dissonance are "modern" and that all "modern" music is dissonant This is a misunderstanding that places contemporary music at a disadvantage. Dissonance in various degrees may be found in music of all ages. Palestrina, Bach, Haydn, Mozart, Beethoven, Tchaikovsky, Chopin, and all the other "favorite" composers of the general public have dissonances in their compositions.

Many are reluctant to give new music a fair trial. This attitude is not new. Debussy's *Prelude to the Afternoon of a Faun* was loved and hated when it was first performed and Stravinsky's *Rite of Spring* was called outrageous. Today both are accepted by audiences all over the world.

Many of Beethoven's first performances were failures, partly because his manuscript was so poorly written that it was difficult to read. The musicians were not very well trained and certainly the theatre lighting must have been next to impossible by our present-day standards.

Today the difficulties that confronted Beethoven do not exist. Stravinsky's manuscript is as neat and exact as printed music. The performers are the finest in history and the lighting is excellent.

Where does the difficulty lie in the failure of a contemporary work that shows up later as a great success? Primarily with the listener; he has a greater responsibility than he realizes. In the first place he must have the proper mental attitude. He must be tolerant and listen to some contemporary works many times before he arrives at a fair evaluation of them in relation to his listening pleasure. Some are not easy to become familiar with and only by familiarity can we expect to comprehend, appreciate, or enjoy new music.

A sympathetic understanding of the literary content of contemporary program music is also very important. Let us consider parts of Samuel Barber's *Medea,* the ballet music supporting the scenes depicting some of the episodes of the Greek legend.

Greek mythology tells of Medea, one of the most fiendish characters ever conceived by the imagination of man. She killed her two sons because she was angry with their father, Jason. Can you imagine Barber depicting this scene with a sweet, singable, sentimental melody?

Composers, critics, and analysts are also partly to blame for widening the gap between the music and the average listener because they often present a scholarly analysis of the music in such a way that only they themselves can understand it. Furthermore they come out with a lot of "isms" in describing the music. They use such terms as futurism, neo-primitivism, neo-mysticism, proletarianism, pseudo-exoticism, utilitarianism, etc. until the average person is so confused and discouraged that he is inclined to give up in despair.

Don't let all this stop you from exploring contemporary music. If you don't enjoy Expressionistic music, the most difficult of all listening, try the many other kinds of music being written today. There are twentieth-century compositions that have all of the characteristics of Romantic music, some have qualities of Impressionism, some have traces of Baroque or Classic ideas, still others have a very strong popular idiom. In other words there is no such thing as a definite type of music that can be called "modern."

Explore new fields of listening occasionally. Your taste changes from time to time. Composers are always looking ahead, exploring new possibilities. They all hope that their music will enjoy successful hearings. The composer is writing for you as well as for himself.

Rarely do we find imitators whose works are as great as those of the innovators. Should we be old-fashioned and rest in the arms of the arts of our grandmothers? Writing a classic minuet is about as absurd as going back to living in a log cabin!

Be an explorer. Endless hours of pleasure are waiting for those who have the right attitude and are willing to take a chance. You will find some musical craftsmanship, some experimentation, some objectivity, some emotional restraint, some emotional emphasis, and endless types and kinds of music. The characteristics of Romanticism that so many people like are to be found in many compositions. Romanticism is never dead!

We would like to call the reader's attention to Neo-Classic music which is very approachable and is one phase of contemporary development that is very heartening to the less experienced listener. Neo-Classicism is a contemporary style of composing which is a return to the eighteenth-century classic point of view as far as clarity, objectivity, balance of form, and transparency of orchestration are concerned. It is a departure from the Classic style of writing in that the melodies and general presentation are in twentieth-century idioms. Clarity, balance of form, and transparency of orchestration are characteristics that tend to make Classic and Neo-Classic music easier to get acquainted with and enjoy.

ABOUT AMERICAN MUSIC

All kinds of music will be found among the compositions by Americans. Some American composers write in a very romantic vein, paying quite a bit of attention to expressive melodies and good psychological form and they are not afraid of being a bit old-fashioned. Others reach out into unexplored realms and new mediums and thus create new types of music.

Great strides are being made in America, looking toward new horizons in all branches of musical endeavor. There is much experimenting. This is always a part of creative activity but occasionally there is a tendency for a few listeners to be artificially carried away with something that they cannot understand so that they may bask in the presence of what appears to be the avant-garde. On the other hand there is the conservative listener who may be too much inclined to avoid the new.

Practically all internationally recognized American music dates from the turn of the century. Musically we are a very young country. The first American to receive European recognition was Edward MacDowell (1861–1908). Others followed slowly but at present there are hundreds of composers who are struggling to be heard.

American works occupy only from 4 to 5 per cent of the programs of most major orchestras and the general public seldom has a chance to get acquainted with a number before it is withdrawn from the repertoire. From the standpoint of the conductors, managers, and committees responsible for financial maintenance of the orchestras, the performance of more new American works or lesser known works is a bit hazardous.

Some of these works may continue to be performed while others may be discarded sooner or later, and the discarded ones may have some influence on music of the future. This is something with which the listener need not be concerned. We are rarely concerned about the future value of a present-day musical show. Just enjoy listening to the music!

In most American music we find that the basic elements have not been ignored by the composers. It takes fine, sensitive, creative ability of considerable stature to write original melodies containing substance, character, and vitality. However there are those who hold that melody is not as important in some contemporary idioms as it was formerly. Emotion, ranging from flagrant to extremely subtle, is a part of the expressive quality in music but some think this is old-fashioned. For some composers, form is psychologically an essential part of music if it is to convey its message in full and yet not overdo an idea in driving home a point, but some feel that content is much more important. With some, splashes of harmonic color or fragments of melody are effective and a part of their style, but others hold that this leads only to chaos. To some, harmony is very important even to the point of conforming to the early traditional, but with some composers other elements become more important.

There is no attempt made here to arrive at any conclusions or make any predictions about American music. With but few exceptions there is no attempt made to classify the composers since they are, for the most part, ruggedly individualistic.

TWENTIETH-CENTURY SYMPHONIES

Barber: Symphony No. 1, Op. 9 (1936; revised 1942)
  In one long movement, this symphony has changes from dramatic to lyric, always with freshness in a Post-Romantic style. The dissonant passages enhance the effectiveness of the lyric sections.
Chávez: *Sinfonia India* (1935–1936)
  This Mexican composer has used authentic Mexican-Indian melodies and rhythms in this one-movement composition which is now listed in some catalogs as *Symphony No. 2.* The themes were collected from among the Seris of Sonora,

the Huicholes of Nayarit, and the Yaquis of Sonora. This composition is appealing to lovers of authentic Mexican music.

Chávez: *Sinfonia Romantica* (Symphony No. 4) (1952–1953)

This symphony is written for a large orchestra and is in three movements—traditional in structure. Just as the title implies this is quite Romantic in style, especially the second movement with its beautiful melodies first by the strings alone and then supported by the brass accompaniment. The orchestration is rather unusual and most effective. The third movement is in a vivacious Mexican style.

Effinger: Little Symphony No. 1 (1945)

This is a Naumburg Award Symphony in four short movements for chamber orchestra. Being natural and unforced is a problem with composers in the twentieth century. Here is an example by a composer who is not afraid to be Romantic. This is light listening—a contemporary "divertimento."

Gould: *Latin-American Symphonette* (1940)

The composer has captured Spanish musical flavor with exotic Caribbean, Negro, and Indian influence in these delightful dances: 1. *Rhumba,* 2. *Tango,* 3. *Guaracha,* 4. *Conga.*

Hanson: Symphony No. 2, "Romantic" (1930)

This symphony in three movements is well named, for it is truly Romantic in every sense of the word. The melodies are beautiful, singable tunes. The entire symphony is very accessible.

Harris: Symphony No. 3 (1939)

This work is one of the few American compositions that has continued in the repertoire of a few major symphony orchestras. It has appeal to both musician and audience; is not very long; has accessible melodies; and is in one movement. Harris has furnished the following program for the four sections of the symphony: Tragic, Lyric, Pastoral, and Fugue.

Hindemith: *Symphony, Mathis der Maler* (1934)

This is a Neo-Classic work made up of excerpts from Hindemith's opera, *Mathis der Maler* (Matthias the Painter) which is based on the life and religious paintings of Matthias Grünewald (*c.* 1460–1528). It is really not a symphony but a suite of symphonic poems that are based on the subjects "Angels' Concert," "The Entombment," and "The Temptation of St. Anthony." The first is happy; the second elegiac; the third depicts the agonizing experiences of St. Anthony but ends in a glorious Hallelujah Hymn.

Ives: Symphony No. 2 (1897–1902)

Here is a symphony for the inexperienced listener and one for the seasoned veteran of many years. Familiar fragments of themes of nineteenth-century composers such as Brahms and Wagner are popping up all over the place. Fragmentary suggestions of old hymn tunes and popular melodies of by-gone days are ever-present. It can be quite a game to pick up a phrase here and there of "comments" or "quotes" from different composers. In the hands of Charles Ives from Danbury, Connecticut, we hear all of these as if we were letting our imagination do a little reminiscing. Most of the time these tunes are not exactly the same as the original but they certainly remind the listener of something that he has heard before.

Janáček: *Sinfonietta for Orchestra* (1926)

This is recognized as the composer's orchestral masterpiece. There is an abundance of brass (the score calls for twelve trumpets). The composer delights in scoring instruments in the extremes of their ranges. The third movement is melancholy—almost like a lament. The melodies are over a very low brass accompaniment. There is considerable Moravian folk-song and folk-dance influence throughout. Parts of the fifth movement sound oriental. This is for those interested in a composition that is neither "modern" nor "old-fashioned."

Nielsen: Symphony No. 5, Op. 50 (1921–1922)

Carl Nielsen, one of Denmark's greatest composers, did not indicate a definite program for this symphony but it is known that he had in mind a musical portrayal of the conflict of World War I. The first of the two movements starts in a mood that is solemn and foreboding. A constant rhythmic pattern by the snare drum is a force that gradually builds up tension. The creative genius of the composer is very evident in the beautiful Romantic melodies. The second and last movement is in four sections. The second section has beautiful polyphonic melodies in the strings, then by the horn and bassoon. The last section depicts turmoil ending in triumph.

Prokofiev: Classical Symphony in D, Op. 25 (1916–1917)

This symphony was written for fun—a sophisticated satire on

Classicism. Among other things we note that Prokofiev did not include the traditional minuet for the third movement but in its place—a gavotte!

Prokofiev: Symphony No. 5 (1944)

This whole symphony is very melodic. It is one of the most popular of all twentieth-century symphonies. It is in Neo-Classic style tending toward the Romantic. The scherzo-like second movement sounds as though it might have been written by a nineteenth-century composer. It is alternately rhythmic and melodic but always dancelike. The poignantly expressive melodies of the slow movement show influences of the times. They are tragic, dramatic, and pleading. Prokofiev called this symphony "a symphony about the spirit of man." It should be in every library.

Schuman, William: Symphony No. 8 (1960–1962)

This symphony was commissioned by the New York Philharmonic to celebrate the opening of the Lincoln Center. It was premiered October 14, 1962. The whole symphony is quite melodic but the harmonic idioms are quite advanced and tend to make it a bit difficult for the listener. In listening to a work of this kind it is well to listen to the melodies and let the rest serve as mood or background. The slow movement has singing melodies ranging from pensive to dramatic with tension built up in the harmony—not the melody. The third and last movement has very interesting polyphonic material and development, also some exciting percussion tonal effects. This symphony is for those who are enthusiastic about contemporary music.

Shostakovich: Symphony No. 5 (1937)

This symphony was premiered November 21, 1937, as a part of the celebration of the twentieth anniversary of the Soviet Republic. It was received with great enthusiasm and is still the most often played of all the works of Shostakovich. It is in four movements. The first is made up of contrasting moods; the second is light and gay; the third is deeply emotional; the last returns to contrasting moods. This is an outstanding and fine example of Neo-Classicism; a composition for those who would like to get acquainted with contemporary music that is not too far out; one they would not tire of quickly.

Thompson: Symphony No. 2 (1931)

A delightful, unforced, agreeable work in popular idioms reminiscent of the 1920's with unmistakable influence or experimentation with ragtime, syncopation, and blues. The fast movements have delightful rhythms, the third movement having 7/4, 6/8, and 9/8 rhythms. The Largo is lush and romantic with its melancholy blues typical of some of the popular music of the "roaring twenties."

Vaughan Williams: Symphony No. 2, "London" (1914; revised 1920)

This symphony, in traditional four movements, was intended to be absolute music. It is so illustrative of London—its fog, the Thames, Westminster, Big Ben, the jolly cockney, and the bustle of a busy day—that a pictorial program has been attached to it. An impression of a day in London starts with the early morning fog and mist, then the city's awakening, the activities of the day, the evening, and then the return to quiet—it is midnight.

Vaughan Williams: Symphony No. 3, "Pastoral" (1922)

A Romantic-Impressionistic musical picture of the English countryside—the serenity of the gently rolling hills—small wooded areas—winding roads—all at peace with the world.

TWENTIETH-CENTURY
MISCELLANEOUS ORCHESTRAL SUITES

Bartók: Music for Stringed Instruments, Percussion, and Celesta (1935)

Bartók did more to explore the musical possibilities of percussion instruments than any other composer. This suite, made up of Andante tranquillo, Allegro, Adagio, and Allegro, is undoubtedly the composer's greatest orchestral work. It varies from subtle sombre moods to the most thrilling rhythmic effects.

Britten: "Four Sea Pieces" from the opera *Peter Grimes* (1945)

1. Dawn, 2. Sunday Morning, 3. Moonlight, 4. Storm.

de Falla: *Nights in the Gardens of Spain* (1909–1915)

1. In the Gardens of the Generalife, 2. Far-off Dance Is Heard, 3. In the Gardens of the Sierra de Cordoba.

This suite is called *Symphonic Impressions, for Piano and Orchestra*. The piano has a very important part in the orchestration but is not a solo instrument as in a concerto. The "Gardens of the Generalife" are gardens near the Alhambra. In the last number you hear a party in progress in the distance, with gypsies playing, dancing, and singing. The whole suite is very festive.

Gould: *Spirituals for Orchestra* (1942) (Suite in Jazz Idioms)
The captivating moods in the various numbers are consistent with their titles, which are: Proclamation, Sermon, A Little Bit of Sin, Protest, and Jubilee.
Grofé: *Grand Canyon Suite* (1931)

1. Sunrise, 2. Painted Desert, 3. On the Trail, 4. Sunset, 5. Cloudburst.

This popular orchestral suite of symphonic poems abounds in Impressionism and Realism with considerable Romanticism to tie it together. "Sunrise" is especially beautiful as the colorful orchestration seems to unfold darkness into dawn and the glories of a new day. The stubborn donkey in "On the Trail" is a good bit of humorous realism. The thunder and lightning with the torrents of rain in "Cloudburst" are so real that you are almost prompted to put up your umbrella.

Hindemith: *Symphonic Metamorphosis on Themes by Weber* (1943)

1. Allegro, 2. Turandot, Scherzo (from incidental music for the German version of a Chinese play), 3. Andantino, 4. March.

This is one of Hindemith's most popular works. It is enjoyed greatly by musician and nonmusician alike.
Holst: The Planets, Op. 32 (1914–1917)

1. Mars, the Bringer of War, 2. Venus, the Bringer of Peace, 3. Mercury, the Winged Messenger, 4. Jupiter, the Bringer of Jollity, 5. Saturn, the Bringer of Old Age, 6. Uranus, the Magician, 7. Neptune, the Mystic.

This romantic suite is written for a very large orchestra with large wind and percussion sections. Every instrument has an important part somewhere in the suite. A women's choir chanting a wordless chorus appears in the Impressionistic "Neptune." The subtitles are a guide for the general character of each number—moods ranging from poetic mysticism to very dramatic and powerful grandiose expression. There is a great wealth of orchestral tone color in these musical characterizations.

Ibert: *Divertissement for Chamber Orchestra*
Introduction, Cortege, Nocturne, Valse, Parade, Finale.

This is a suite taken from Ibert's incidental music for *"Le Chapeau de paille d'Italie."* It was written for fun and is witty, irresistible, refined, musical humor. No thinking—just relax and listen.

Ibert: *Escales* (Ports of Call) (1922)

Elusive musical impression of three Mediterranean ports of call—Palermo, Tunis, and Valencia—developed out of three tunes heard on a voyage. The music is a lush combination of Impressionism and Romanticism.

Ives: *Three Places in New England* (1903–1914)

Sometimes referred to as *A New England Symphony,* this suite has the following titles: The "Saint Gaudens" in Boston Common; Putnam's Camp, Redding, Connecticut; The Housatonic at Stockbridge. Ives' creative genius is exemplified in these musical pictures. Repeated listening and close study of these pieces will open up a new world for the conscientious rugged explorer. Only recent years have brought an appreciation of this composer. He was far ahead of his time. The following lines are from a poem which is a preface to the first picture:

"Moving—Marching—Faces of Souls!
Marked with generations of pain,
Part-freers of a Destiny,
Slowly, restlessly—swaying us on with you
Towards other Freedom!"

In the second musical picture we hear two bands each marching toward the center of the town from opposite directions, each band playing a different march. The resultant clash of sound can hardly be imagined. The third number is a musical setting of a New England countryside, inspired by a walk through meadows along the river near Stockbridge.

Kodály: *Hary Janos Suite* (1926)

1. Prelude—The Fairy Tale Begins, 2. Viennese Musical Clock, 3. Song, 4. The Battle and Defeat of Napoleon, 5. Intermezzo, 6. Entrance of the Emperor and His Court.

This descriptive suite from the comic opera, *Hary Janos,* is an example of Hungarian nationalistic music. The "Intermezzo" is a czardas, a traditional Hungarian folk dance. The hero, Hary Janos, is a vain braggart who claims he defeated Napoleon single-handedly.

Schuman, William: *Credendum* (Article of Faith) (1955)

1. Declaration, 2. Chorale, 3. Finale

This was commissioned in 1955 by the United States National Commission for UNESCO through the U.S. Department of State. It was the first time that the U.S. Government commissioned a symphonic composition. The opening section which is primarily for wind instruments and percussion is very impressive and dramatic. In the "Chorale" we hear Romantic melodies that are very expressive and singable. The "Finale" is full of cheerful, scherzo-like material. Singing melodies are interspersed with exciting, contrasting, dancelike material and brought to a close with a thrilling climax.

Taylor: *Through the Looking-Glass*

The full orchestral version of this humorous suite is dated 1922. It continues in the repertoire of some orchestras as a perennial favorite. The suite, named after Lewis Carroll's story by the same name, contains the following: 1 a. Dedication, 1 b. The Garden of Live Flowers, 2. Jabberwocky, 3. Looking-Glass Insects, 4. The White Knight.

TWENTIETH-CENTURY CONCERTI

Barber: Concerto for Piano and Orchestra, Op. 38 (1962)

This was commissioned by the music publishers G. Schirmer, Inc., New York. The first performance took place September 24, 1962, during the week of the Lincoln Center inaugural. In 1963, Samuel Barber was given the Pulitzer Prize for this concerto. It is one of the most outstanding works of its kind by any contemporary composer. It is a striking example of a major twentieth-century composition showing an amalgamation of influences of the past and present. It has had many performances both here and abroad and is a most welcome addition to the repertoire.

Bartók: *Concerto for Orchestra* (1944)

In essence this is a symphony. It was commissioned by Serge Koussevitsky, conductor of the Boston Symphony Orchestra, and completed just a year before Bartók died. The whole composition is full of melodies—idioms that were quite personal with the composer—influences of his native Hungary—folk songs and dances. The last movement is east-European music deluxe! The five movements are: Introduction, Game of Couples, Elegy, Interrupted Intermezzo, and Finale. Bartók himself had this to say about his *Concerto for Orchestra:* "The general mood of the work represents, apart from the jesting second movement, a gradual transition from the sternness of the first movement and the lugubrious death song of the third to the life-assertion of the last one."

Bartók: Concerto No. 3 in e minor, for Piano and Orchestra (1945)

This concerto, Bartók's last composition, is a masterful conclusion to a very productive life. It has in it many musical ideas that were typical of the composer throughout his career. Free and varied rhythms in the first and last movements with expressive melodies in the second are all created in quite traditional form. This is an outstanding contribution to twentieth-century music.

Gershwin: Concerto in F for Piano and Orchestra (1925)

This popular concerto was commissioned by Walter Damrosch, then conductor of the New York Symphony Society. Damrosch specified that it was to be a jazz piano concerto. It is full of jazz syncopated rhythms and "blues" melodies that were in vogue during the "roaring twenties." This concerto remains in the current repertoire despite the fact that the type of jazz that inspired the work is no longer popular but considered "old-fashioned."

Imbrie: *Concerto for Violin and Orchestra* (1950–1954)

This concerto was commissioned by the Koussevitsky Foundation, dedicated to the memory of Serge and Natalie Koussevitsky, and was given a Naumburg Award. This is one of the few violin concertos of note by an American composer in recent years. It abounds in contemporary idioms and, like many compositions of our times, there are many sections that seem to have too much going on at the same time. The welcome lyrical passages are very effective because of the contrast. The listener would do well to listen to melodic lines and let the rest be "background." It is only for the advanced listener.

Khachaturian: *Concerto for Piano and Orchestra* (1936)

This brilliant popular work has considerable exotic flavor. The second movement is rather melancholy in contrast to the gymnastic third movement, which sweeps on to a grand theatrical conclusion.

Poulenc: *Concert Champêtre for Harpischord and Orchestra* (1927–1928)

This unusual concerto was written for Wanda Landowska,

world-renowned harpsichordist, at her request. It is in Neo-Classic style and true to its title which means "Rustic Concert." The second movement is a sweet and charming melodic Andante. At times, the last movement is reminiscent of compositions by Baroque composers. The harpsichord is transplanted into the twentieth century in an exciting setting. If you are at all interested in the harpsichord do not miss this one.

Poulenc: *Concerto for Organ, Strings, and Timpani* (1938)
Accessible contemporary organ compositions are hard to find. Here is one of which the average listener, with some experience with contemporary idioms, need not be afraid.

Poulenc: *Concerto in d minor for Two Pianos and Orchestra* (1932)
This is for those who are interested in contemporary music that is not hard work to listen to. Poulenc is not afraid to compose music for the sake of music. It is always delightful and never complicated—absolutely unforced.

Prokofiev: Concerto No. 3 in C for Piano, Op. 26 (1921)
Prokefiev made his reputation on this concerto. It is still recognized as one of his best works. It is not difficult for the inexperienced listener even at first hearing. It is in Neo-Classic style—melodic—changing moods—brilliant at times—always sustaining interest.

Prokofiev: Concerto No. 2 for Violin, Op. 63 (1935)
Noteworthy violin concertos are hard to find among the compositions of the twentieth century. This is one that can stand up among the best of them. Prokofiev never loses sight of the fact that the violin is a singing instrument and that it is also capable of expressing the full gamut of emotion.

Rodrigo: *Concierto de Aranjuez for Guitar and Orchestra* (1940)
This is a full scale work in three movements. It is most unusual—full of Spanish spice—excellent—of high interest to those interested in the Spanish guitar at its best!

Shostakovich: Concerto for Piano, Trumpet and Orchestra, Op. 35 (1933)
This is an exciting composition and a rather unusual combination. It is typical Shostakovich style with flavors of popular idioms. Whether the Soviets like it or not this Russian composer has been influenced by American jazz music.

Shostakovich: Concerto for Piano and Orchestra, Op. 101 (1957)
This is not a profound work. Jolly themes and exciting

rhythmic patterns in the first movement are followed by the beautiful, stately, romantic melodies of the Andante. The third movement has delightful rhythmic and technical fireworks. This concerto is very easy to listen to yet it wears well.

TWENTIETH-CENTURY
MISCELLANEOUS MUSIC FOR
SOLO INSTRUMENT AND ORCHESTRA

Bloch: *Schelomo*—Rhapsody for Violoncello and Orchestra (1916)
This is one of the most widely played and best known of the works of Bloch. Hebraic melodies of varying moods are fluently fashioned, one after the other. Accessible at first hearing.

Britten: Symphony for Cello and Orchestra, Op. 68 (1963)
First performed in 1964, this "Symphony" is written so that the cello and orchestra are of equal importance. It is scored with the orchestra playing in both the high and low registers and a thin transparent orchestration in the middle register so that the cello is heard at all times. The first movement in classic sonata-allegro form is in a rather advanced melodic and harmonic idiom. The second is a playful scherzo with sections that are eerie and then pensive. The exquisite third movement has a brooding melody—conversations between the cello and timpani—duet with cello and horn—later interspersed with brass. The cadenza for the cello is occasionally punctuated by remarks from the timpani. The last movement, "Passacaglia," has great variety. This symphony is good listening for the contemporary enthusiast.

Dohnányi: *Variations on a Nursery Theme* (1913) (Piano and Orchestra)
The composer's most popular work. It is a series of witty variations in Romantic style, on a tune to which many, in years past, learned the alphabet.

Gershwin: *Rhapsody in Blue* (1924)
This is not the first but one of the first compositions in a jazz idiom. It is a perennially popular favorite among those interested in easy listening.

Rodrigo: *Concert-Serenade for Harp and Orchestra* (1954)
This serenade is made up of the following: 1. Estudiantina: Allegro, 2. Intermezzo: Molto tranquilo, 3. Sarao: Allegro-deciso. The first movement is bubbling over with a carefree,

youthful, carnival spirit. The second is plaintive with a meditative melody and has a sprightly middle section. The third movement is very festive, lighthearted and dancelike. Anyone interested in Spanish music will enjoy this one.

Schuman, William: *A Song of Orpheus* (1960–1961)
This fantasy for cello and orchestra is based on the composer's song, "Orpheus With His Flute," which he wrote in 1944. The text of the song from Shakespeare's "Henry VIII" is written in with the cello score to assist in interpretation. It goes back and forth from a singing, romantically emotional style to tense contemporary idioms.

Stravinsky: *Movements for Piano and Orchestra* (1958–1959)
This, as are most of the other later works of Stravinsky, is rather difficult to listen to. These five very short movements are partly related to serial forms that are discussed in Chapter 11.

TWENTIETH-CENTURY
MUSIC FOR PIANO SOLO
AND SMALL ENSEMBLES

Barber: Sonata for Cello and Piano, Op. 6 (1932)
This is the work of a young composer. This sonata, in three movements, is a very enjoyable romantic composition.

Bartók: "Sonata for Two Pianos and Percussion" (1937)
This is an exciting adventure for those who are looking for something unusual. The percussion effects are extraordinary.

Milhaud: *Scaramouche Suite for Two Pianos* (1937)
This is a perennially popular favorite with two-piano teams and audiences alike—the irresistible encore type. The last number, "Brazileira," a samba, was inspired by the composer's Brazilian experiences. Scaramouche is a literary character described as "Born with a gift of laughter and a sense that the world was mad."

Prokofiev: Sonata for Violoncello and Piano, Op. 119 (1949)
This is not a profound work but one that is full of a chain of lyrical melodies that are sad, pensive, mysterious, or happy. The second movement is jovial and youthful while the first and third are melodic with a Romantic character.

Prokofiev: "Piano Sonatas" (9) (1912–1947)
Numbers one and two are good starters. If you have not heard these you have a treat in store. Traces of Impressionism may be found in Sonata Number 2.

Shostakovich: Piano Quintet, Op. 57 (1941)

There is very little twentieth-century chamber music of high calibre or even chamber music that commands more than a passing interest. This quintet is a twentieth-century masterpiece in this form. It is Neo-Classic with madrigal-like texture—singing polyphonic melodies. These change to contemporary idioms still retaining the polyphonic style with dignity. The scherzo has popular appeal while the fourth movement shows the genius of the composer in the beautifully created sublime melodies. The last movement is humorous with a jolly popular appeal that is not banal in the slightest.

Shostakovich: Sonata for Violoncello and Piano, Op. 40 (1934)

This is Neo-Classic in design and melodic style—in traditional form with restrained expressive melodies. In the second movement we have a charming, buoyant waltz with the piano and cello constantly exchanging "comments." The third movement is a sorrowful, deeply moving cello melody. The last movement is playful and happy with a technically difficult, rapid, middle section. Lovers of chamber music should not be without this sonata.

Varèse: "Ionisation" (1931)

This piece requires thirteen players. It is written for thirty-seven percussion instruments ranging from conventional to exotic.

TWENTIETH-CENTURY BALLET MUSIC

Barber: *Medea* (Ballet, "Cave of the Heart") (1946)

1. Parados, 2. Choros—Medea and Jason, 3. The Young Princess—Jason, 4. Choros, 5. Medea, 6. Kantikos agonias, 7. Exodus.

A fine musical characterization of Medea and Jason, and the general atmosphere surrounding the episode depicting uncontrollable jealousy, and the horror of Medea's revenge in cruel fiendish murder.

Bernstein: *Fancy Free* (1944)

This very gay and animated suite is easy listening. It is cast in a mixture of contemporary popular idioms with considerable Latin-American accent.

Copland: *Billy the Kid* (1938)

The story is about the outlaw, Billy the Kid. Cowboy tunes, carefree rhythms, and musical impressions of the wide-open spaces remind us of the "gun-totin' " pioneer days.

Falla: *Amor Brujo, El* (Love, the Magician) (1915)

1. Introduction and Scene, 2. The Gypsies—Evening, 3. Scene of Sorrowing Love (with vocal solo), 4. The Homecomer, 5. Dance of Terror, 6. The Magic Circle, 7. Ritual Fire Dance, 8. Scene, 9. Song of the Will-o'-the-Wisp (with vocal solo), 10. Pantomime, 11. Dance of the Game of Love (with vocal solo), 12. Morning Chimes.

This is superb Spanish music with French Impressionistic influence. It is a pantomime ballet, but with vocal solos sung off-stage. Sometimes, in the orchestral suite, the numbers containing vocal parts are left out, or the voice parts are taken by instruments in the orchestra.

Khachaturian: *Gayne,* Ballet Suite No. 1 (1942)

1. Sabre Dance, 2. Dance of Aysche, 3. Dance of the Rose Maidens, 4. Dance of the Kurds, 5. Lullaby, 6. Dance of the Young Kurds, 7. Armen's Variations, 8. Lezghinka.

Everyone seems to know the "Sabre Dance" but the rest of this suite is equally interesting. If you like part of the suite you will like all of it.

Milhaud: *Le Création du Monde* (1923)

This is the first piece of serious music to be written in the jazz idiom. The ballet, with its Negro settings, was first performed in Paris by a Swedish Ballet. If you want to see what jazz idioms were like in the "roaring twenties," listen to this one.

Piston: *The Incredible Flutist* (1933)

In 1940, the suite, abridged by the composer himself, was first performed by the Pittsburgh Symphony Orchestra. It is divided into twelve episodes as follows: 1. Introduction, 2. Dance of the Vendors, 3. Entrance of the Customers, 4. Tango, 5. Entry of the Circus, 6. Circus March, 7. Solo of the Flutist, 8. Minuet, 9. Spanish Waltz, 10. Eight O'Clock, 11. Siciliano, 12. Polka Finale.

Prokofiev: *Cinderella* (1941–1944)

The story of lovable Cinderella by Charles Perrault (1628–1703) does not need to be recounted here. The music is light listening, filled with lyrical content, and excitingly descriptive. With the ballet it becomes excellent theatre. Without the ballet it is good "dinner music."

Stravinsky: *L'Oiseau de feu* (Firebird) (Original, 1910)

The story is a mixture of several fantastic Russian fairy tales. Ivan, our hero, finds himself in a mysterious forest. He captures an enchanted golden feathered bird—the Firebird—but soon releases it and is rewarded with a single magic golden feather. Fair maidens warn Ivan of demons, a magician and his castle, and the possibilities of being turned to stone. Ivan and the Firebird join forces and overcome the magician and all the evil spirits. In return, Ivan is given his choice of the maidens. There are three orchestral suites made from this ballet. The third has (according to Stravinsky) "short pantomimic episodes" between sections so that it flows in unbroken sequence. It is called the "new augmented version."

Stravinsky: *Petrouchka* (1911)

The plot of this ballet revolves around an oriental-appearing Charlatan and three animated dolls: Petrouchka, a Ballerina, and a Moor. A puppet love affair ensues—Petrouchka is thwarted and refused by the Ballerina—the wicked Moor entices the Ballerina—the Ballerina encourages the Moor—the Moor kills Petrouchka—the ghost of Petrouchka haunts the Charlatan.

Stravinksy: *Le Sacre du printemps* (The Consecration of Spring) (1913)

This is for the rugged listener only. Its symphonic version is divided into two sections: 1. The Adoration of the Earth (Introduction: Harbingers of Spring; Dance of the Adolescents; Spring Rounds; Games of the Round Cities; The Procession of the Wise Men; Adoration of the Earth; Dance of the Earth); 2. The Sacrifice (Introduction; Mysterious Circles of the Adolescents; Glorification of the Chosen One; Evocation of the Ancestors; Ritual of Ancestors; Sacrificial Dance of the Chosen One).

TWENTIETH-CENTURY INCIDENTAL MUSIC

Copland: *The Quiet City* (1940)

This is an adaptation of the incidental music that Copland wrote for the play by the same name. Interesting solo parts by the trumpet and the English horn set the general mood of this rather brooding piece depicting loneliness in the city.

Prokofiev: "Alexander Nevsky," Op. 78 (1939)

The composer calls this a cantata. It is for those who like bold, stirring vocal and orchestral music. The setting for the historical film, for which the music was originally written, is dated 1242. This is an excellent example of music for films. In listening to this work, one should imagine himself a part of this thirteenth-century drama.

Stravinsky: *L'Histoire du Soldat* (1917–1918)

This suite is from the music for the play by C. F. Rasmuz, a Swiss novelist. Early Stravinsky compositions are easy listening. This one has been popular throughout the years. The titles of the various numbers of the suite are: 1. The Soldier's Story, 2. Soldier at the Brook, 3. Pastorale, 4. The Royal March, 5. The Little Concerto, 6. Three Dances: Tango, Waltz, Ragtime, 7. The Devil's Dance. 8. Chorale, 9. Triumphal March of the Devil.

Thomson: *Louisiana Story* (1948)

This music was awarded the 1949 Pulitzer Prize. The semi-documentary film by Robert Flaherty is concerned with the effect of oil wells and mechanization on the Acadians living in the bayou region in Louisiana.

Thomson: *The Plow That Broke the Plains* (1936)

This suite is from the score for the Pare Lorentz documentary film concerning soil conservation. The titles are: Prelude, Grass, Cattle Songs, Blues, Drought, Devastation.

Vaughan Williams: Symphony No. 7, "Sinfonia Antartica" (First performed in 1953)

(Orchestra, superscriptions, soprano voice, and wordless chorus) Prelude, Scherzo, Landscape, Intermezzo, Epilogue. The superscriptions are from the pens of Shelley, Coleridge, and Donne, an extract from Captain Scott's Diary, and a portion of Psalm 104.

This "Sinfonia" originated in Vaughan Williams' music for *Scott of the Antarctic,* the film which deals with Robert Falcon Scott's fatal 1912 exploration of the mysteries of the great white wilderness of the Antarctic. The musical impression of the heroic struggle to conquer the wastelands of the polar regions is tremendously impressive.

This is one of the most powerful musical pictures ever portrayed. The orchestration is magnificent. The music abounds in haunting ethereal effects, sudden surprises, ominous sounds—and then . . . terror! The explorers suddenly confront an impassable ice fall! The futile struggle against the savagery of nature in the blizzard is depicted with superb artistry.

Villa-Lobos: *Forest of the Amazon*

This suite of very descriptive music for symphony orchestra, chorus, and soprano soloist is one of the composer's last works. It was taken from the incidental music which he wrote earlier for the film production of Hudson's "Green Mansions." The setting of the book is in the Orinoco Plains in Venezuela but Villa-Lobos chose to call the suite *Forest of the Amazon*. The suite is made up of the following: Deep in the Forest, Excitement Among the Indians, Nature's Dance, Savage War Dance, Sails, On the Way to the Hunt, Twilight Song, Indians in Search of the Girl, Head Hunters, Blue Dusk, Love Song, and Forest Fire.

TWENTIETH-CENTURY
MISCELLANEOUS INSTRUMENTAL MUSIC

Barber: "Adagio for Strings" (1936)

This is a beautiful, short lyric piece in romantic style, arranged by the composer from the slow movement of his String Quartet, Op. 11.

Barber: "Essay for Orchestra, No. 1" (1938)

This is melodic and singable like the "Adagio." The first and third parts are slow. The middle section is a scherzo-like allegro. The whole piece is unquestionably romantic. This is beautiful music for the conservative listener.

Bartók: "Divertimento for String Orchestra" (1939)

This spirited and sparkling composition is one of the most genial of all of the compositions of this composer.

Chávez: "Toccata for Percussion" (1942)

One of the most exciting pieces written for percussion alone. The composer uses everything in the pantry.

Copland: "El Salon Mexico" (1936)

This is an excellent musical impression of Old Mexico. The composer has captured Latin-American idioms in rhythms and spirited melodies. Here is fifteen minutes of irresistible entertainment.

Enesco: "Roumanian Rhapsody, No. 1" (1907)

A popular piece which is made up of various Roumanian melodies, ranging from sentimental to bold and boisterous.

Gershwin: "American in Paris" (1928)

A musical picture of an American's impressions, while taking a walk down the Champs Élysée in Paris. The moods change in this symphonic poem as we hear impressions of French taxicabs, cafés, a church, an attack of homesickness, the

Charleston, gayer moods and then . . . well, let's make the most of it. This is Paris!

Hindemith: Theme and Four Variations, "Four Temperaments" (1940)

1. Theme, 2. Melancholic, 3. Sanguine, 4. Phlegmatic, 5. Choleric—these make up the titles of this composition. It is scored for piano and string orchestra and written in a Neo-Classic style. This is an excellent example of the composer's style in 1940.

TWENTIETH-CENTURY OPERAS

Barber: *Vanessa*

This opera was first performed at the Metropolitan in 1958. Since then it has been produced abroad and has been rather successful despite its somewhat shallow plot. The libretto was written by Menotti. The music is quite accessible melodically.

Britten: *Peter Grimes* (1945)

Peter Grimes was first performed in 1945. The libretto of this opera in three acts is taken from George Crabbe's *Borough* (1810), a story of life in Borough, an English fishing village. Peter Grimes, a fisherman, is a maladjusted villager. Things just go from bad to worse until he accepts the advice of a friend who tells him that it is best he go out to sea in the storm.

Gershwin: *Porgy and Bess* (1935)

This is an American folk opera, Gershwin's last major work. Some of the popular songs in this opera are "Summertime," "I got plenty of nuttin'," "You is my woman now," and "My man's gone now."

Menotti, Gian Carlo

Menotti's musical shows are all effective theatrical productions. The style is a fusion of Romantic, Impressionistic, and Contemporary idioms. *Amahl and the Night Visitors* is best known and best loved of all. The tragedies are difficult listening at first but the theatrical side is so tremendous that they soon "get under your skin."

Amahl and the Night Visitors (TV Christmas chamber opera) (1951)

Amelia Goes to the Ball (1937) (One-act comic opera)

The Consul (1950) (Musical drama—a tragedy in three acts)

The Medium (1946) (Musical drama—a tragedy in two acts)

The Old Maid and the Thief (1939) Comic opera originally for radio—then for TV)

MISCELLANEOUS TWENTIETH-CENTURY VOCAL MUSIC

Barber: Andromache's Farewell, Op. 39 (1963)
This is a powerful dramatic song for soprano. It portrays an episode in Euripides' tragedy "The Trojan Women." Troy is captured by the Greeks. The young son of Andromache, daughter-in-law of the queen, is sentenced to be thrown from the top of the highest wall of Troy. This is a mother's farewell to her son. It was written for the celebration of the opening of the Lincoln Center in New York City in 1963.

Bloch: *Israel Symphony* (1912–1916)
This program symphony is in three sections: Adagio molto ("Prayer in the Desert"), Allegro agitato ("Yom Kippur"), Moderato ("Succoth"). The symphony, starting and ending with prayer-like plaintive passages, is neither "modern" nor "old-fashioned." In the last movement, two sopranos, two altos, and a bass, placed among the instruments of the orchestra, sing the deeply moving strains, "In Thee I trust" and "Thou art my refuge."

Bloch: *Sacred Service* (1933)
This is a Jewish choral service—a masterpiece. Another work of the composer that it not intended to be "modern." However, it does have changing rhythms, unusual melodic lines and twentieth-century harmonic style but all blended in with traditional presentation of the text. It is more difficult listening than the *Israel Symphony.*

Britten: *Ceremony of Carols* (1942)
This is a beautiful cycle of Christmas songs in Neo-Classic style for women's voices with harp accompaniment. Besides the processional and recessional there are eight carols for solo voice, duet, or chorus and a harp solo, "Interlude."

Britten: *Les Illuminations,* Op. 18 (Tenor and Orchestra) (1939)
The artistry and creative genius of Britten are evident throughout this cycle as in his "Serenade." *Les Illuminations* is made up of: Fanfare, Villes, Phrase, Antique, Royauté, Marine, Interlude, Being Beauteous, Parade, and Depart. The poems are by the French poet, Jean Rimbaud.

Britten: Serenade for Tenor, Horn and Strings, Op. 31 (1953)
The artistic combination of tenor solo and French horn, the sympathetic string accompaniment, and the atmosphere

created in this song cycle make it an outstanding work. It is made up of the following: Prologue, Pastorale (Cotton), Nocturne (Tennyson), Elegy (Blake), Dirge (Anon.), Hymn (Ben Jonson), Sonnet (Keats), Epilogue.

Britten: *War Requiem* (1962)

This unusual Requiem is scored for soprano, tenor, and baritone soloists; chorus; boys' choir; organ; and orchestra. Britten skillfully combined the traditional Latin Mass with poems by Wilfred Owen, a young English poet who lost his life in World War I. Owen wrote: "My subject is War, and the pity of War. The Poetry is in the Pity. All a poet can do today is warn." Some of the lines of the poems are: "What passing-bells for these who die as cattle?"; "Bugles sang, sadd'ning the evening air"; "Out there, we've walked quite friendly up to Death"; and, "I am the enemy you killed, my friend." This is not the red-blooded patriotic hero who dies in battle for love of his country but a humane, poetic point of view—the futility of war.

Foss: *Time Cycle* (1957)

The texts of the four songs in this cycle are *We're Late* by W. H. Auden, *When the Bells Justle* by A. E. Housman, "From Franz Kafka's Diaries—January 16" and "O Man! Take Heed!" from Friedrich Nietzsche's *Thus Spake Zarathustra.* Now tonal, now atonal, now the music is more important, now the words are more important, now accessible, now far out, now the music is composed, now it is improvised, now an orchestra, now a chamber ensemble, now in English, now in German . . . reflections on life, death, solitude, eternity . . . "the clocks do not synchronize . . ."

Honegger: *Le Roi David* (King David) (1921)

This oratorio is scored for soloists, narrator, chorus, and orchestra. The various vocal parts—including many Psalms—are connected by way of the narrations which tell of the events in the life of David. This deals primarily with his rise from humble state to king.

Janáček: "The Diary of One Who Vanished" (1916)

In this song cycle for tenor soloist with piano accompaniment, the text—which is of unknown origin—is a poetic diary of a young man who relates the story of his love affair with a gypsy girl. It is made up of twenty-two songs. An alto soloist takes the part of the gypsy girl in numbers nine, ten, and eleven and women's voices are added to make it more realistic. The cycle illustrates Janáček's ability to blend *Sprechgesang* (speech-song) and folk music.

Janáček: *Missa Glagolitica* (Slavonic Mass) (1926)

This was written to be a part of the celebration of the tenth anniversary of the Czechoslovak republic; it is a festival concert, not a work intended for a religious service. The text is similar to the Latin but in the language of the area of Czechoslovakia in which Janáček lived. The Mass begins with an orchestral Introduction and ends with an orchestral *Intrada* or conclusion. Between the *Agnus Dei* and the *Intrada* is a rugged organ solo. This is a powerful work for every choral enthusiast.

Kodály: *Te Deum* (1936)

This glorious, colorful, outstanding composition ranges from a plaintive, chant-like melody to massive choral and orchestral effects. Kodály's *Te Deum* runs an emotional gamut. The text of the *Te Deum* was a favorite among seventeenth- and eighteenth-century composers. This one, with its Hungarian nationalistic flavor, is a match for any of them.

Orff: "Carmina Burana" (Songs of Beuren) (1936)

This is a collection of twenty-five songs with texts by goliards (wandering scholars), poets, and monks of the thirteenth century. This work must not be confused with a recently recreated authentic version. We think that these songs were originally a part of some sort of theatrical production. Orff's version is spectacular with popular rhythmic and melodic appeal.

Poulenc: Mass in G (1937)

This is a beautiful choral work that lasts about twenty minutes. The composer has conveyed devotional impact in a contemporary style that is rather unusual.

Stravinsky: *Symphony of Psalms* (1930)

One of the great works of the twentieth century, this is an outstanding example of Neo-Classicism. The last part—the magnificent setting of the Psalm of praise, Psalm 150—should be heard first. After becoming well acquainted with this, listen to the whole work. The double fugue may be a little difficult at first but after several hearings you will be greatly rewarded for your time and effort.

Villa-Lobos: *Bachianas Brasileiras* No. 5 for Soprano and 8 Celli

Everyone should know this composition. The *Bachianas* is an invention of Villa-Lobos. It is a melodic and polyphonic composition in a form similar to what Johann Sebastian Bach might have written, but different in that the melodies and general atmosphere are just what you would expect of Latin American music.

ELECTRONIC MUSIC

Electronic music is the newest adventure in sound. The first public concert in the United States of music for tape recorder was at the Museum of Modern Art, New York, in 1952.

Many sound mediums are used to create electronic music for tape recorders. Those working in the field do not hesitate to record any kind of sound, whether it be conventional or otherwise. It may be a recording of an orchestral instrument or human voice. It may be the sound of rain, a dripping faucet, trains, doorbells, thunder, city traffic, a vacuum cleaner, sirens, squealing brakes, or anything that makes a sound, soft or loud.

These sounds may be changed in any number of ways. The pitch can be changed by slowing up or speeding up the recording. For instance a recording of the timpani, when speeded up, will have a very high pitch—a timbre that could not be produced in any other way. A gradual change of speed will make a sustained sound slide either up or down. The dynamic level of any given sound can be changed at will, either slowly or rapidly. Fundamental pitches or any overtones of any sound can be sifted out for use in a recording. Any alteration of any sound can be exact.

Furthermore, any number of altered or unaltered sounds may be superimposed one upon the other. The possibilities are unlimited. Many times it is impossible to recognize the origin of the sounds created while other sounds are obvious.

Suggested Electronic Music:

Luening and Ussachevsky: *Suite from* King Lear (1956)
Otto Luening and Vladimir Ussachevsky collaborated in this creation. This suite is made up of two excerpts from the abstract incidental music for Orson Welles' production of Shakespeare's "King Lear." The first part, the storm, is quite realistic with clashing, howling sounds and the second, King Lear's madness, is full of weird and eerie sound effects.

Varèse: *Poème Électronique* (1958)
This is perhaps the most unique of all the works of Varèse. It was designed to provide continuous sound for the Philips Radio Corporation's pavilion at the Brussels Exposition. The sounds are often weird and unearthly.

Varèse is often referred to as one of the greatest experimenters in sound. He objected to having his work called "experimental" since, as he said, the experimenting has been done and now it is up to the listener to experiment.

Chapter Thirteen

MUSIC FOR
WIND INSTRUMENTS

THE SMALL brass ensemble dates back to the days of the early Roman empire when groups of brass players were called upon to play fanfares and the like to call attention to some important announcement or event.

From the latter part of the Renaissance to the early Classic period considerable music for brass instruments was written for religious services. During the seventeenth century, music was written for brass ensembles to be played from towers. For example, the brass ensembles by Johann Pezel listed below were written for town musicians who played from the Rathaus tower in Leipzig, Germany. They played twice daily, at 10:00 A.M. and 6:00 P.M.

As far as major composers were concerned, there appears to have been little interest in wind ensembles during the Romantic period. However, at the turn of the century, we find that the concert band, through its high artistic accomplishments, has attracted the attention and interest of many outstanding composers both here and abroad.

The list of suggested music for wind instruments includes many different styles of writing. The list is organized according to periods to assist the interested listener. Comments are made only when there are points that may interest the reader or be helpful in his choice of music. We suggest that you refer to the general characteristics of music of the various periods while looking for material.

RENAISSANCE

Gabrieli, Giovanni (1557–1612): "Canzoni from *Sacrae Symphoniae*"

The *Sacrae Symphoniae*, a collection of various types of music for use in the church service, was published in 1597. The "Canzoni" are for double brass ensembles (two groups of players). This was very effective in St. Mark's Cathedral, Venice, where they had two pipe organs and two galleries. One group of brass players would play in one gallery and the second group would play in the other. These are excellent in stereo recordings.

BAROQUE

Chamber Music

Pezel, Johann (1639–1694): "Sonatas for Five Brass Instruments"

Quantz, Johann Joachim (1697–1773): Trio Sonata in c minor (for Flute, Oboe, Bassoon, and Harpsichord)

Stölzel, Gottfried Heinrich (1690–1749): Trio Sonata in c minor (for 2 Oboes, Bassoon, and Harpsichord)

Concerti

Manfredini, Francesco (*c.* 1680–1748): *Concerto for Two Trumpets and String Orchestra*

Torelli, Giuseppe (1658–1709): Concerto in D Major for Trumpet and String Orchestra

Miscellaneous

Handel: Royal Fireworks Music

The original scoring for the first performance in 1749 was for 9 trumpets, 9 horns, 24 oboes, 12 bassoons, and 1 contrabassoon (one of the first performances for this instrument, new at that time), timpani, and drums.

Stölzel: *Concerto Grosso for Trumpets, Woodwinds, Strings, Harpsichord*

This is listed here because of the important parts that the trumpets and woodwind choir have. It is an outstanding composition by a composer who is not very well known. It has the grandeur of true Baroque.

PRE-CLASSIC

Bach, J. C.: Sinfonia No. 2 in B flat Major (for 2 Clarinets, 2 Horns and Bassoon)

Haydn: Three Divertimenti: G Major, D Major, and C Major

These lighthearted suites for 2 oboes, 2 horns, and 2 bassoons were written about 1760 when Haydn was employed by Count Morzin at the Lubavec castle.

Mozart: Five Divertimenti in B flat Major, K. 229 (1783)
These divertimenti for 1 oboe, 1 clarinet, and 1 bassoon are delightful "dinner music."

Telemann, G. P.: *Concerto for Three Trumpets, Timpani, Two Oboes, String Orchestra, and Harpsichord*
This is in concerto grosso style in the first, second, and fourth movements. The third movement, "Largo," is a beautiful oboe solo in classic style with string accompaniment.

CLASSIC
Chamber Music

Beethoven: Quintet in E flat Major, Op. 16 (Piano, Oboe, Clarinet, Bassoon, Horn)

Mozart: Quintet in E flat Major, K. 452 (Piano, Oboe, Clarinet, Bassoon, Horn)

Concerti

Haydn: Concerto in E flat for Trumpet and Orchestra
Of value to those interested in the trumpet. It is one of the best concerti for trumpet.

Mozart: Concerto in A Major for Clarinet and Orchestra, K. 622
This is one of the finest of its kind.

Mozart: Four Concerti for Horn: No. 1 in D Major, K. 412; No. 2 in E flat Major, K. 417; No. 3 in E flat Major, K. 447; No. 4 in E flat Major, K. 495
All the concerti listed here should be in every library.

Miscellaneous

Haydn: "March for the Prince of Wales"
Seven marches have been authenticated as having been written by Haydn including the "Hungarian National March," two in E flat Major, two for the Derbyshire Cavalry Regiment, and one which he called *March Regimento de Marshall.*" These marches are scored for various combinations of clarinets, oboes, bassoons, horns, trumpets, and serpent (obsolete bass brass instrument—part usually taken by the tuba). The percussion instruments of Haydn's time which included timpani, bass drum, cymbals, and triangle

are not written in the score but are to be improvised by the percussionists. These marches were written during the last decade of the eighteenth century.

Mozart: Serenade in B flat Major, No. 10 for Wind Instruments, K. 361

Mozart: Serenade in E flat Major, No. 11 for Wind Instruments, K. 375

Mozart: Serenade in c minor, No. 12 for Wind Instruments, K. 388

These entertaining suites are scored for from six to thirteen instruments. In these three "Serenades" we have some of the finest music ever written for wind ensembles.

ROMANTIC

Schumann: *Konzertstück* for Four Horns and Orchestra
Schumann became interested in the new valve horns. The *Konzertstück* grew out of this interest. It is scored for 2 horns with valves, 2 horns without, and orchestra.

TWENTIETH-CENTURY
Band

Barber: "Commando March" (1943)
Hanson: "Chorale and Alleluia" (1953)
Harris: *Symphony for Band* (1938)
Hindemith: Symphony in B flat for Band (1951)
Holst: Suite No. 1 in E flat, Op. 25a (1909)
    Chaconne, Intermezzo, March
Holst: Suite No. 2 in F, Op. 28b (1911)
    March, Song Without Words, Song of the Blacksmith, and Fantasia on "Dargason"
Mennin: "Canzona for Band"
Persichetti: "Psalm for Band" (premiered 1952)
Reed: *La Fiesta Mexicana* (1956)
    Prelude, Mass, Festival
Stravinsky: *Symphonies of Wind Instruments* (1920)
Thomson: *A Solemn Music* (1949)
Vaughan Williams: *Folk Song Suite* (1924)
    March: Seventeen Come Sunday, Intermezzo: My Bonny Boy, March: Folk Songs From Somerset
Vaughan Williams: *"Toccata Marziale"* (1924)

Chamber Music

Berezowsky: Brass Suite, Op. 24 (1939)
Dahl: "Music for Brass Instruments" (1944)
Hindemith: *Morgenmusik* (1932)
Sanders: Quintet in B flat (1942)
Stravinsky: "Octet for Wind Instruments" (1922)

Miscellaneous

Hindemith: Concert Music for Strings and Brass, Op. 50 (1930)
This is scored for 4 horns, 4 trumpets, 3 trombones, and tuba.
To this, Hindemith stated that he wanted added "the strong-
est possible string quartet." By this he meant a full orchestral string choir. This was written for the Boston Symphony
Orchestra when they were celebrating their fiftieth anniversary. It was played by the Boston Symphony for the first time
in 1931. It is very thrilling festive music that should be in
the library of every brass enthusiast.

Chapter Fourteen

MUSIC APPRECIATION
IN THE HOME

MUSIC FOR CHILDREN

NEVER in history has any country spent so much money on music in secondary schools and colleges as we do in the United States today. Most of it is spent on participation which is only a starter on the road to appreciation.

Participation is one thing and appreciation is another. This is as true in music as it is in all of the other fine arts: drama, ballet, movies, radio, and television. The person who plays a horn is no more capable of enjoying piano music than the person who has never played a musical instrument.

In music, participation and listening may go along hand in hand, or they may be developed separately. The performer must do considerable listening but very often his listening becomes specialized in the line of his participating interests.

The place to start music appreciation is in the home. There is no "right way" to introduce a child to music as a listening art. One "system" may be advisable in one home and not in another. We hope that some of the following suggestions will be helpful.

Taking time for a little music does not need to be a chore, because so many excellent recordings are designed to acquaint children with the instruments of the orchestra; the structural form of the symphony; program music; and many other first-rate musical productions. These are so well done that the entire family can enjoy them together.

A record player of quality is one of the first considerations.

This is quite important. You cannot expect a child to be happy with an old discarded portable record player very long. How is he going to be able to get acquainted with the sound of orchestral instruments unless he gets accustomed to their true timbre? How is he going to get the feeling that enjoying good music is a part of gracious living if he is pushed off into his own room to play old beaten-up records and hillbilly stuff? This has its place but also has its limitations.

For the smaller child, a little music in the evening is an excellent substitute for the good-night story. Music for the child at bedtime and music for mother and father afterwards does not need to disturb the child's sleeping habits. If this is routine, it may even get to the point where he requests music for a few minutes so that he may be able to go to sleep. Regular habits like this give him a sense of comfort and a feeling that all is normal—all is well.

Various children's recordings are designed for different age levels. These age levels are not infallible. It depends upon the amount of listening experience and the interest of both the child and the parent. For example, it is not impossible or unusual for a child of six or seven to be able to identify all of the instruments of the orchestra. This study must continue, however, or, like all other forms of early education, the child will lose this ability.

Children love pictures along with their records and their listening. Choose fine children's records with good illustrations and acquaint the child with two arts at the same time.

There are very fine recordings of nursery rhymes and songs. Introduce the children's versions of symphonic tone poems, ballets, etc., from time to time. *Hansel and Gretel, Sleeping Beauty, Swan Lake, Peer Gynt,* "The Night Before Christmas," and many others are available. Record companies are aware of the importance of this feature and are constantly improving the quality of their output.

Listen to original versions of program music with your child during this picture stage. Start with a short tone poem, or part of a suite that you know very well. Tell the whole story about the music first and then have a "running" commentary along with the music so that the child will know what is going on. A little acting or impersonating won't hurt.

In painting word pictures of the music, the parent develops his own imagination along with the child's and a feeling of closer personal relationship is brought about. Present-day home life is apt to grow into activities for individual members of the family.

Listening to music can be interesting and inspiring to all.

If music has been a part of family life, it can be a great source of entertainment for a child when he is confined because of illness. It is not wasted effort to have good music on the radio or record player when the children are playing on the floor or playing quietly at some game. You may not be aware of it but some of it will make a lasting impression.

The following symphonic poems and descriptive suites are good starters in the field of program music for the whole family. These symphonic poems, individual numbers in the suites and movements of the symphonies, are rather short. This is important because the child's listening span is very limited. Suites with variety are desirable because the change in tempo and mood refreshes the interest. The record covers will have complete stories of the symphonic poems and suites. It is up to the parent to be well acquainted with the music so that he may explain what is going on while listening.

For ideas about listening to symphonic poems, refer to page 72. The starting ages mentioned in the suggested list vary with the amount of listening experience.

Suggested Symphonic Poems for Children (start at age 8 to 12):

Dukas: *Sorcerer's Apprentice*
> The apprentice gets into trouble because he did not know the magic word to stop the broom from carrying water—the whole place was flooded!

Liadow: *Baba Yaga*
> The old witch flies through the air to her hut on the mountaintop.

Saint-Saëns: *Danse Macabre*
> Children love the xylophone imitating the rattle of bones— the oboe representing the rooster crowing at dawn—the skeletons scuttling back to their graves.

Greig: *Peer Gynt* (see page 80)

Kodály: *Hary Janos* (see page 121)

Mussorgsky: *Pictures at an Exhibition* (see page 75)

Prokofiev: *Winter Bonfire*—Children's Suite
> This suite has two names, "Winter Bonfire" and "Winter Holiday." It is a good one to arouse interest in listening because the music is related to something that the child can understand readily. There is a great deal of realism. For instance, the very first number, "Departure," starts out with the orchestra making sounds like a train. The titles will give

145

you a general idea of the contents of the suite. They are: Departure, Winter Night, Waltz on the Ice, The Bonfire, Song of the Boys, Evening Around the Stove, March, The Return.

Tchaikovsky: *The Nutcracker Suite*

This is a ballet with a Christmas story about a little girl who received a nutcracker as a Christmas gift. In her dream the nutcracker turned into a fairy prince who escorted her to see the various scenes interpreted in the ballet. See page 21.

Saint-Saëns: *Carnival of the Animals*

For family fun, get the version with poems about the animals by Ogden Nash. The suite was written as a bit of humor and Nash's poems are a captivating addition to the original. See page 75.

ACQUAINTING CHILDREN WITH THE INSTRUMENTS OF THE ORCHESTRA

It can be very interesting and easy for children to learn to identify the instruments of the orchestra by their timbre. Very fine compositions and recordings have been made especially for this purpose. These vary in content and age level. Only those that seem to be permanently available are listed.

Often, there is a desire to discuss the music during or immediately after the playing of a record. It is advantageous in such discussions to be acquainted with the timbre of the various instruments. Some children get a great deal of satisfaction out of just being able to identify the instruments without any outside motivation.

As a record is being played, it is interesting to look for the picture of the instrument that you are listening to and note its position in the orchestra. Refer to the illustration of the orchestral instruments, seating chart, and other ideas in Chapter 2. Children in junior high and senior high school will be interested in the recordings by Britten and Hanson mentioned near the end of the chapter. For the younger listener, as well as for all ages, the following is recommended:

Prokofiev: *Peter and the Wolf* (with narrator)

This is recommended for listeners from age eight to eighty. In this story, different instruments represent people, animals, and birds. The flute represents the bird; the clarinet—the cat; the oboe—the duck; the bassoon—the grandpapa; etc. This composition has always been a great favorite.

THE CHILD AND THE SYMPHONY

It is not easy to interest a very young child in a symphony by a major composer. Sometimes it is advisable to wait for a time until there has been considerable interest developed in program music. When the child shows an interest in program music you might try Goldmark's Rustic Wedding Symphony, Op. 26. The program of the four movements are "Wedding March," "Bridal Song," "Serenade," and "In the Garden."

The following plan has been found to be successful. Interest the child in "Viennese Musical Clock" from Kodály's *Hary Janos Suite*. Relate all of the fantasy surrounding the story of Viennese clocks that have figures that appear at the hour and do all sorts of things just like puppets. After some time elapses, play the slow movement from Haydn's "Clock" symphony and note how similarly the clock idea is carried out by a much earlier composer. Keep in mind that children learn to like absolute Classic music much more quickly than other types of absolute music. Try them out on Haydn's Symphonies Nos. 6, 7, and 8 ("Morning," "Noon," and "Evening").

Some children take to the *Toy Symphony* by Leopold Mozart. This is the symphony that was formerly erroneously attributed to Haydn. It is a short conventional symphony played by two violins, double bass, piano, and a lot of toys: drum, trumpet, rattle, quail, cuckoo, and nightingale.

GLOSSARY

THIS GLOSSARY is made up of terms used in this handbook; those often used in general conversation about music; and those commonly found in program notes. It is not intended to be a complete music dictionary nor is it intended to deal with the terms except in their general usage in this book. Very often a term has different meanings depending upon (1) the period in music history with which it is associated, e.g., "sonata," (2) the commonplace or the learned usage, e.g., "classic," (3) the literary, scientific, or musical meaning, e.g., "dynamic." All definitions have been simplified as much as possible so as to avoid confusion. For further and more detailed information we suggest that you refer to the latest edition of a reliable complete dictionary of music.

Absolute Music. Music in which the composer presents various moods that have no literary or pictorial program.

A cappella. A song sung without accompaniment.

Antiphonal. Two groups of musicians singing or playing alternately.

Aria. A song for solo voice that is a part of a major work such as an opera, oratorio, or a cantata.

Art Song. A song of high artistic quality for solo voice. The text is usually a very fine lyric poem supported by or fused with a sympathetic accompaniment. The German Art Song or *Lied* made its appearance with Franz Schubert's lieder (pl.)

in the early nineteenth century. These songs of Schubert are with piano accompaniment. Later some composers used an orchestral accompaniment, e.g., the Art Songs of Gustav Mahler. See pages 84 and 103.

Atonal. Literally without a key but more accurately applied to its general usage in referring to music composed by means of the "twelve-tone technique" or method of composing with all of the twelve tones within the octave. This is a great departure from the traditional Classic and Romantic approach. See page 106.

Ballet. An artistic theatrical dance, performed by a group of dancers in appropriate costumes, to the accompaniment of music. See page 77.

Baroque. A period in art history that dates quite definitely from 1600 to 1750. The music of the period is in general serious, with an abundance of polyphonic as well as homophonic literature in which the listener may expect well-defined melodies and regular rhythms. See page 32.

Baroque Solo Concerto. A composition with considerable polyphonic treatment written for a solo instrument and orchestra. See page 35.

Baroque Suite. A group of antique dances. See page 35.

BWV (Bach Werke Verzeichnis). Catalog numbering of the works of J. S. Bach, e.g., Bach: "Sonata for Flute and continuo," BWV 1035.

Cadenza. A section of a composition for solo voice or solo instrument that is written in free style giving the soloist a chance for considerable technical display. Compositions where cadenzas are most commonly found are the Classic and Romantic concertos and very often operatic arias, particularly those for soprano.

Cantata. A vocal work with either sacred or secular text for solo voice(s) and chorus, usually with orchestral accompaniment. See Bach cantatas, page 46.

Chaconne. A composition that has a "ground bass" which is normally used as a basis for the harmonic structure. See *Ground Bass* and *Passacaglia.*

Chamber Music. Generally thought of as music for a small group of instrumentalists that was originally intended to be performed for small audiences in rather intimate surroundings—not a *large* concert hall. See page 82.

Chanson or *French Chanson.* Early French songs that are predominantly homophonic but still with some polyphony. The general character of the music is closely associated with the spirit of the text. See page 27.

Choir of the Orchestra. A body of instruments in the symphony orchestra having some common trait or characteristic such as the string choir, woodwind choir, brass choir, or percussion choir. See page 5.

Chorale. A reformation term given to a hymn to be sung by the church congregation in the language of the people. See page 41.

Chorale Prelude. An organ composition based on the tune of a chorale. See page 42.

Classic. In ordinary and deteriorated usage the term Classic seems to be applied to any music that appears to be first-rate. In this book the term is used in connection with Haydn, Mozart, and Beethoven. It should be noted that the later works of Beethoven are more Romantic in character than those of either Haydn or Mozart. For a more thorough discussion see page 58.

Coda. A sort of conclusion or "epilogue" found at the end of a composition such as in the sonata-allegro form. See page 62.

Codetta. A semiending at the end of a section of a composition.

Color. Color in music is the psychological interpretation of the quality of sound produced by any instrument(s), voice(s), device(s), or any combination thereof. See (7) page 4.

Comic Opera. Same as Opéra Comique.

Concertante or *Concertato Style.* Contrasting or pitting vocal or instrumental parts against each other.

Concertino. The solo group in the Concerto Grosso. See page 37.

Concerto. In general, a composition for solo instrument and orchestra. With but few exceptions the classic construction of the solo concerto, with its three movements (fast, slow, fast) and cadenzas, has been retained since the time of Mozart. See page 65.

Concerto Grosso. This type of concerto differs from the concerto in that there is a *group* of solo instruments and the entire orchestra. It should not be confused with concertos written for two solo instruments, such as Brahms' *Concerto for Violin, Cello, and Orchestra* which is called a "double concerto," nor concertos written for three solo instruments, such as Beethoven's *Concerto for Violin, Cello, Piano, and Orchestra* which is called a "triple concerto." See page 37.

Continuo. The part played by a keyboard instrument in an ensemble to fill in the harmonic and polyphonic structure. See *Trio Sonata.*

Contrary Motion. One or more voices in the harmonic or polyphonic structure moving in the opposite direction to one or more other voices.

Contrapuntal (adjective). In the style of counterpoint.

Counterpoint. Literally, melody against melody. The simultaneous use of two or more melodies, each having specific significance.

Crescendo. Gradually increasing in volume.

Cyclic, Cyclical. A term used loosely to denote any musical form which has a number of movements such as a sonata, symphony, or suite. More specifically, a composition that has some unifying element, either programmatic or thematic, in each of the movements, e.g., Beethoven's *Pastoral Symphony* and Berlioz' *Symphonie Fantastique.*

Development. Unfolding of the thematic materials in a composition by inversion, elaboration, fugal treatment, various combinations of themes, etc.

Diminuendo. Gradually decreasing in volume.

Divertimento. This term implies music that is a pleasing diversion. The term was used by composers like Mozart to mean a suite of pleasant pieces.

Dynamics. Volume. See (5) page 4.

Elements of Music. The elements of music are: rhythm, melody, harmony, tempo, dynamics, form, and color. See page 3.

Ensemble. A group of two or more musicians.

Exoticism. Exoticism in music may be described as musical culture not characteristically European or Western.

Exposition. In a fugue, any section in which the main subject or tune has appeared in all voices or positions. In sonata-allegro form—the section where the main subjects or themes are first presented. See pages 40 and 61.

Expressionism. A radical trend in modern music which started during the second decade of the twentieth century. It deals with abstractions—a definite departure from the conventional. The term is a borrowed one. It was first attached to such painters as Picasso, Dali, and Klee. See page 105.

Family of Instruments. A group of instruments that produce their musical sounds in the same way and have somewhat the same timbre and appearance.

Form. The design or structure of a composition. See (6) page 4.

Fugue. A contrapuntal composition with a certain number of voices—usually three or four—written according to certain rules. See page 39.

Gregorian Chant. A monophonic liturgical song, in free rhythm, that is used in the Roman Catholic Church. These chants were named after Pope Gregory (590–604).

Ground Bass. A rather short bass melodic line that is repeated over and over with different harmonic structure and upper melodies for each repetition—often erroneously called "variation." See *Passacaglia* and *Chaconne.* Ground bass is also known as "ostinato."

Harmony. Chordal structure or a combination of tones that are sounded simultaneously. See (3) page 3.

Homophonic. Music with a single melody and accompaniment.

Idiom. In music an idiom may be rather loosely defined as being a language or style of composing.

Impressionism. A school of composers in the late nineteenth and early twentieth century (principally Debussy and Ravel) who directed their attention and interest toward vagueness in music. See page 93.

Incidental Music. Music played before or during the action of a play to assist in establishing, supporting, or intensifying the mood of the drama. See page 79.

Inversion. A theme is said to be inverted when it is turned upside down.

K. (Köchel). A numbering system by Dr. Ludwig, Ritter von Köchel for cataloging the works of Mozart, e.g., *Jupiter Symphony,* K. 551. See Op. (Opus) and L. (Longo).

Key. A family of tones bearing a definite relation to each other.

L. (Longo). A numbering system by Allesandro Longo for cataloging the works of Domenico Scarlatti, e.g., "Cat Fugue," L. 462.

Leitmotif (German spelling: Leitmotiv). Literally this means "leading motif" or a guiding feature in a musical composition or extended work such as an opera. Musical themes or motifs are attached to recurrent ideas, to characters, things, events, or states of being in the production. This technique was used extensively by Wagner in his operas. The term *leitmotif* was coined by one of his friends.

Libretto. A text of a long major work such as an opera, oratorio, or cantata. Usually the operatic libretto has the original language and a translation.

Lied (pl.: lieder). A German Art Song. See *Art Song.*

Madrigal. In general, an unaccompanied polyphonic song with a secular text. See page 26.

Mass. A commemoration of Christ's sacrifice on the cross. For complete text of the Ordinary, see pages 27, 28.

Melismatic. Two or more (often many) notes sung to one syllable. The term melismatic is used more correctly in connection with the Gregorian chant than with any other vocal literature.

Melody. A tune. See (2) page 3.

Mixed Rhythms. Frequent changes of rhythm in one composition.

Monophonic. A single, unaccompanied melody.

Motet. In general, an unaccompanied polyphonic song with a sacred text. See page 26.

Motive, Motif (German, *Motiv*). A fragment of a melody.

Musical Review. Somewhat like an operetta except that very often there is no continuous plot.

Mute. A clasp that is placed on the bridge of a member of the violin family to give it a quiet, sombre, and sort of mysterious timbre. Also a pear-shaped device which is inserted in the bell of a brass instrument. It not only softens the volume but changes the timbre.

Nationalism. Nationalism in music may be rather loosely defined as music showing the traits or characteristics of native folk music, dances, and the general culture of the people of a particular country.

Neo-Classicism. A contemporary style of composing which is a return to the eighteenth-century classic point of view as far as clarity, balance of form, and transparency of orchestration are concerned. It is a departure from the classic style in that the melodies, harmonies, and general presentation are in twentieth-century idioms.

Op. (Opus, Latin). The abbreviation of the term opus (work) is used in conjunction with figures (Op. 1, Op. 2, etc.) to number the works of a composer. A number is usually assigned to a composition by the composer but in some cases the number is assigned by the publisher. The numbers most often indicate the order in which the compositions were written.

Opera. A drama set to music, either tragic or comic, very often sung throughout. In an operatic production we expect first-rate singing, scenery, costumes, staging, and orchestra. Occasionally there is a little spoken dialogue and in some operas the composer and librettist have chosen to include ballet.

Opéra Bouffe (French). Same as Opéra Comique.

Opera Buffa (Italian). Same as Opéra Comique.

Opéra Comique (French). Although there are exceptions, opéra comique is generally an opera with a rather light plot, some spoken dialogue, and a happy ending. Comedy often plays an important part and the whole production is more accessible than an opera.

Operetta. A musical comedy with considerable spoken dialogue. The production is not as lavish as an opera. The plot usually appeals to the audience because of its preoccupation with the contemporary scene. Many plots are satirical and have various implications.

Opus (Op., Latin). Work. See *Op.*

Oratorio. A vocal work with an extended libretto which is usually of a religious character. In an oratorio we can expect choruses, solos, duets, etc., with orchestral accompaniment. It is usually designed to be sung without costumes, scenery, or action.

Orchestral Tone Color. Tone color of a combination of orchestral instruments. It is usually thought of in connection with a combination of instruments of different timbre.

Ordinary of the Mass. That part of the Mass that remains constant throughout the church calendar or church year.

Ostinato. See *Ground Bass.*

Overture. There are three different kinds of overtures. They are: 1. Operatic Overture—an orchestral introduction to an opera or similar work, 2. Incidental Overture—an orchestral preface to a play, and 3. Concert Overture—an independent concert piece for orchestra. See page 76.

Pantonal. A term used by Arnold Schönberg that means "inclusive of all tonalities." Schönberg did not use the term "atonal" which, in substance, means the same thing.

Parallel Motion. Two or more voices in the harmonic or polyphonic structure moving in the same direction keeping the same distance apart.

Parody Mass. Not a travesty but a Mass based on pre-existing musical material. For example Dufay's Mass: *Se la face ay pale* (If my face is pale) is based on the tune of a song by the same name.

Passacaglia. An instrumental composition which has a "ground bass" normally in the bass but it may appear in any of the upper voices.

Percussion. The percussion choir of an orchestra or band is made up of instruments that produce sound when struck, for example, drums, triangle, etc. See pages 18, 20, 21.

Pizzicato. Plucking the strings of a stringed instrument with the fingers instead of using a bow.

Plainsong. Similar to a Gregorian chant in that it refers to a monophonic, liturgical song in free rhythm but, in its broadest sense, includes the same kind of music of other Christian liturgies such as Anglican and Greek Orthodox as well as non-Christian, e.g., Jewish and Hindu.

Polyphonic. Two or more melodies played or sung simultaneously.

Polyrhythm. The simultaneous use of two different rhythms. See page 108.

Polytonality. Two or more tonalities heard simultaneously. See page 108.

Post-Romantic. The Romantic period is generally confined to the nineteenth century. A few twentieth-century composers continue to write in a somewhat Romantic style. Generally these composers may be called Romanticists or Post-Romanticists. However, the term Post-Romanticism in music applies more specifically to the music of composers who placed even greater emphasis on emotional qualities than their predecessors. These composers also developed greater tone color in orchestration and used more advanced twentieth-century harmonic idioms. The approximate dates of Post-Romanticism are from 1890 to 1945. See page 100.

Program Music. Music in which a composer wishes to portray or present some literary or pictorial idea through the music.

Proper of the Mass. That portion of the Mass which changes with the church calendar or the liturgical year, such as Christmas, Easter, etc.

Realism. Musical effects that sound like something real, such as wind, storm, etc.

Recapitulation. A restatement of the theme. Sometimes refers to a repetition of the exposition. See Recapitulation in the Sonata-Allegro form, pages 60, 61, 62.

Recitative. For solo voice, usually to be sung in a rather free style as far as rhythm and expression are concerned, placing emphasis on the text. Often syllabic with one note to a syllable in irregular rhythms that become rather speechlike in sound. In an opera it is quite often used as a connecting link between arias, choruses, etc.

Renaissance. A period in art history from approximately 1400 to 1600. Music of this period is quite predominantly polyphonic. See page 26.

Reprise. Like the term "Recapitulation," "Reprise" has several meanings depending upon the period of the music in question. For all practical purposes, to avoid pedantic confusion, Recapitulation and Reprise may be thought of as being synonyms.

Requiem. A Mass for the dead.

Review. See *Musical Review.*

Ripieno. In the Concerto Grosso, the ripieno is the entire orchestra. See page 37.

Rhythm. For all practical purposes rhythm is regular recurring accents or beats. See (1) page 3.

Rococo. A period in art history extending approximately from 1700 to 1775. Rococo music is generally characterized as being graceful and charming with qualities of pleasantness and elegance. See page 52.

Romantic. A period in music history generally including the entire nineteenth century, especially the last seventy-five years. Most of the music of the first twenty-five years is definitely Romantic in character but some, especially the last works of Beethoven (1770–1827), are transitional in character, having qualities of both the Classic and the Romantic. See page 59.

Rondo, Rondo Form, Rondo-Sonata Form. A structural form in which we have unity created by a recurring theme (A-B-A-C-A-B-A). There are several kinds of Rondos but generally speaking it refers to a form somewhat more extended than the Ternary Form (A-B-A) and one that has balance. See page 62.

Scale. A family of tones having a definite relation to each other and written or played in ascending or descending order. Scales are generally made up of all or some of the following intervals: half steps, whole steps, and step and a half.

Serenade. This term implies night-music. It was used by composers like Mozart to mean a suite of pieces.

Serial Music. Music written with a "tone-row" or a "series" as a basis. See page 107.

Similar Motion. All voices moving in the same direction but not necessarily keeping the same distance apart as in parallel motion.

Singspiel (German). The ancestor of German Romantic opera. The German equivalent of Opéra Comique. See *Opéra Comique.*

Sonata. The term was first used during the Renaissance period. It was then used very loosely to indicate any instrumental music in contrast to vocal music which was for the most part referred to as "cantata" or music to be sung. Generally, from the Classic period on, the term "sonata" refers to an instrumental solo, e.g., for piano, for violin, etc. In its broadest sense the term is used to denote a structural form. For details of the classic sonata see The Classic Symphony page 60.

Sonata-Allegro Form or *Sonata-Form.* These two terms are identical. The structural form used in the first movement of a typical classic sonata. In this book the term "Sonata-Allegro form" is used to avoid confusion between Sonata-Form and the Sontata. For detailed discussion see page 60.

Sonata da Camera (chamber sonata). Somewhat like the Baroque "sonata da chiesa" but more flexible in number of movements and content. The camera-type was intended for salon music for small audiences. See page 38.

Sonata da Chiesa (church sonata). The idealized type during the Baroque period is in four movements, slow-fast-slow-fast, and intended for use in a church service. See page 38.

Song Cycle. A series of Art Songs having some psychological association with each other, the same general character, or some general unifying element that makes the entire collection an entity.

Staccato. A very short note.

Suite. A general term applied to any group of compositions intended to be performed one after the other.

Syllabic. One note to a syllable in a vocal work.

Symphonic Poem. An orchestral composition in free form, designed by the composer to present certain literary or pictorial ideas. The form of the composition is usually determined by the pictorial or literary content. See page 72. The Symphonic Poem is sometimes referred to as a Symphonic Tone Poem.

Symphony. A sonata for symphony orchestra. See page 60.

Tempo. The speed at which a composition is performed. See (4) page 4.

Ternary Form. A form made up of two sections, the first called "A" and the second called "B." The pattern of the Ternary Form is generally A-B-A but is quite often A-A-B-A.

Terraced Dynamics. The sudden shifting back and forth from one level of dynamics to another.

Theme. A melody or musical idea. The same as the subject used in a fugue or a sonata. See pages 40 and 60.

Timbre. The quality of color of the sound of an individual instrument or human voice, e.g., various instruments and voices, when sounding the same pitch, have different qualities.

Toccata. A keyboard composition in free style in the idiom of the instrument for which it was written.

Tone. A sound that has regular vibrations giving it a definite pitch.

Tone Color. The psychological association of sound and color. See Glossary definitions of "color" and "timbre."

Tone-Row. All the twelve pitches within the octave, arranged in some arbitrary sequence, and used as the basis and source of material for an entire composition. The tone-row is also known as "series." See page 107.

Transparency of Orchestration. Orchestral music in which the listener can quite readily distinguish each and every instrument(s) or family(ies) of instruments.

Trio. A composition for three voices or three instruments. The term is sometimes used to designate the middle section of a Ternary Form. See page 62.

Trio Sonata (sonata a trè). The typical Baroque trio sonata was written for two instruments having melodic importance and a continuo. The continuo in the trio sonata is a part for a keyboard instrument usually with a string instrument doubling the bass part. Therefore the Baroque trio sonata is usually played by four instruments—not three.

Tutti. In the Concerto Grosso the tutti is the entire orchestra. See page 37.

Twelve-Tone Technique. A method of writing music, using all twelve chromatic pitches in a "tone-row." See page 107.

Variations. A theme is first presented in a rather straightforward manner. It is then modified and embellished in any number of ways. These are called variations. All variations retain the essential features and have something in common with the theme. Sometimes the association between theme and variation is rather obvious while in another variation this association may be quite obscure.

Whole-Tone Scale. A scale made up of whole steps, six equal intervals to the octave.

ITALIAN TERMS FOR SPEEDS

THE FOLLOWING is a list of some of the most commonly used Italian terms which indicate tempi or speeds of various movements of the sonata or other compositions. This listing is from slow to fast.

 Grave—the slowest tempo in music
 Largo—very slow
 Adagio or Lento—slow, a little faster than Largo
 Andante—fairly slow
 Andantino—a little faster than Andante
 Moderato—moderately fast
 Allegretto—fairly fast
 Allegro—fast
 Vivace—lively, faster than Allegro
 Presto—very fast
 Prestissimo—as fast as possible

Other terms modify these tempo terms, such as:

 Allegro assai—very fast
 Allegro non troppo—fast but not too fast
 Allegro con brio—fast with fire
 Allegro moderato—fast with moderation
 Tempo di menuetto—speed of a minuet
 Andante cantabile—fairly slow in a singing style
 Andante tranquillo—fairly slow and tranquil
 Andante con moto—fairly slow with motion

 These universal terms as well as the notation and other indications for interpretation are understood by musicians over the world.

SUGGESTED READING

American Music
>*America's Music,* Gilbert Chase—McGraw-Hill, New York.
>*Modern Music Makers,* Madelein Gross—E. P. Dutton and Co., New York.

Appreciation
>*An Introduction to Music,* Martin Bernstein—Prentice-Hall, Inc., New York.
>*An Introduction to Music,* David D. Boyden—Alfred A. Knopf, New York.
>*The Enjoyment of Music,* Joseph Machlis—W. W. Norton, New York.

Bells
>*Bells of All Nations,* Ernest Morris—Robert Hall, Limited, London.
>*The Carillon,* Frank Percival Price—Oxford University Press, London.

Biographies
>*American Composers Today,* David Ewen—H. W. Wilson Co., New York.
>*Composers of Yesterday,* David Ewen—H. W. Wilson Co., New York.
>*European Composers Today,* David Ewen—H. W. Wilson Co., New York.
>(These three books contain biographies and short discussions of composers' music and lists of principal works.)

Chamber Music
>Chamber Music, Homer Ulrich—Columbia University Press, New York.

Composers' Letters and Writings About Music
>Composers on Music, Sam Morgenstern—Pantheon Books, Inc., New York.

Dictionary
>Harvard Dictionary of Music, Willi Apel—Harvard University Press, Cambridge, Mass.

Encyclopedia of Music
>Groves Dictionary—St. Martin's Press, New York.

Form in Music
>Foundations of Music, Wayne Barlow—Appleton-Century-Crofts, New York.
>The Structure of Music, Robert Erickson—Noonday Press, New York.
>What To Listen for in Music, Aaron Copland—McGraw-Hill, New York.

History of Music
>A History of Western Music, Donald Jay Grout—W. W. Norton, New York.

Instruments of the Orchestra
>The History of Musical Instruments, Curt Sachs—W. W. Norton, New York.
>The Story of Musical Instruments, H. W. Schwartz—Doubleday, Garden City, N.J.

Jazz
>Hear Me Talkin' to Ya, Nat Shapiro and Nat Hentoff—Holt, Rinehart and Winston, New York.

Opera
>Operas and Musical Comedies, J. Walker McSpadden—Thomas Y. Crowell Co., New York.
>A Short History of Opera, Donald Jay Grout—Columbia University Press, New York.

Organ

The Contemporary American Organ, William Harrison Barnes—J. Fischer and Bros., New York.

Piano

Literature of the Piano, Ernest Hutcheson—Alfred A. Knopf, New York.

Program Notes

Analytical Concert Guide, Louis Biancolli—Doubleday, Garden City, N.J.

Masterworks of the Orchestral Repertoire, Donald N. Ferguson—University of Minnesota Press, Minneapolis, Minn.

Pronunciation

NBC Handbook of Pronunciation, James F. Bender—Thomas Y. Crowell Company, New York.

Recorded Music

Guide to Long-Playing Records—Alfred A. Knopf, New York.

Vol. 1. *Orchestral Music,* Irving Kolodin.

Vol. 2. *Vocal Music,* Philip L. Miller.

Vol. 3. *Chamber and Solo Instrument Music,* Harold C. Schönberg.

How To Build a Record Library, Howard Taubman—Hanover House, New York.

The High Fidelity Magazine, The Magazine for Music Listeners, The Publishing House, Great Barrington, Mass.

Symphony Orchestra and Symphonic Music

The American Symphony Orchestra, John H. Mueller—Indiana University Press, Bloomington, Indiana.

Symphonic Music, Homer Ulrich—Columbia University Press, New York.

Twentieth-Century Music

Introduction to Contemporary Music, Joseph Machlis—W. W. Norton, New York.

Music Since 1900, Nicholas Slonimsky—Coleman-Ross Co., New York.

SUGGESTIONS FOR INSTRUCTORS
AND LISTENERS

THIS BOOK is written chronologically so that the reader may have an overall picture of the historical development of music and may more readily find the kind of music that may interest him. It is suggested that the inexperienced listener begin with the most accessible music found among the works of most of the composers of the Romantic period (nineteenth century). Then, look over the listings in the chapter on Rococo and Pre-Classic music. Music of this type is good preparation for music of the Classicists. Along with this, some of the twentieth-century music that is listed as easy listening would be in order. From then on, try earlier music of the Baroque and Renaissance periods, and then the more difficult contemporary music.

It is suggested that the instructor devote the first class period to a brief outline of the historical development of music with a short illustration of each period or phase of development. This will give the student a better picture of the entire course.

The suggestions listed here are not intended to be followed in the order presented but are presented as ideas that may be interesting and helpful from time to time. Just keep in mind that we all have the ability to enjoy all kinds of music. The power of great music is limited only by the ability of the listener to respond.

SUGGESTIONS

1. Musical terms must be defined if we expect to think and speak of music intelligently. Especially is this true of forms such

as Art Song, Symphony, Symphonic Poem, Opera, Oratorio, etc.

2. Dates of periods are important in finding various kinds of music. These dates should be associated with the characteristics of the periods and the composers of each period. This will give the student an overall picture of music as it has developed.

3. Make particular note of important composers of various periods. Associate them with their contribution to the development of music and with the general characteristics of their music.

4. Note that some periods have quite definite beginnings and endings while most of them overlap.

5. Comparing pictures, paintings, and music that depict the same subject can be done much more effectively by slides projected on a screen than by looking at pictures in a book because the listener seems to be more a part of the "scene." Examples are: Monet's *Westminster and Houses of Parliament* and *Waterloo Bridge* with Vaughan Williams' First Movement of "London" Symphony; Toulouse-Lautrec's *Ballet Dancers* with Debussy's *Danse sacrée* and *Danse profane;* a photo of St. Peter's Square in Rome with Monteverdi's *Laudate Dominum.*

6. Pictures of Baroque and Rococo paintings, architecture, interiors, portraits, gardens, etc. are very helpful in creating response to the spirit of the music.

7. Developing the imagination of the listener is a very valuable part of early training; it should always be encouraged. This can be developed by trying to relate what you "see" when you hear a piece of program music which you have never heard before. It is just as well if you do not know what the composer had in mind.

8. Note the growth of the orchestra in number and kind of instruments from its earliest appearance to the present time.

9. Note the predominance of string instruments in early music and the invention, perfection, and development of other kinds of instruments and their influence on composers and their compositions.

10. Identifying instruments by their timbre and by sight adds pleasure, satisfaction, and interest for many listeners.

11. Compare the orchestral tone color of works of Bach, Mozart, Tchaikovsky, Debussy, Schönberg, and various twentieth-century composers.

12. Note the development of music for a particular instrument such as the pipe organ, piano, clarinet, French horn, drums, etc. This study should include the physical development of the instruments, such as development of valves for brass instruments;

materials used in woodwinds, piano, percussion; etc. All these developments relate to the music itself. Except for string instruments the performer is able to do more with present-day instruments than formerly.

13. Compare various periods and schools of development by means of their varied characteristics.

14. Make note of the period during which a particular form or type of music came into being such as Opera, Symphony, Art Song, Symphonic Poem, etc. This is most helpful in locating these forms. Note also the change in these various forms, the style and general characteristics of the music from one period to the next.

15. Forms such as Ternary, Rondo, Variations, and Sonata-Allegro, when understood, are a listening aid and should be thought of only in connection with listening. After all, they are as psychologically sound in structure as the plays of Shakespeare.

16. Counterpoint can easily be understood by noting the counterpoint in Liszt's *Les Préludes* as analyzed in the chapter on Romanticism and relating it to the Bach fugues.

17. The instructor may find it valuable to emphasize some important compositions resulting from the musical and cultural developments preceding the composer.

18. After a study of the Romantic Art Song the Arias of Romantic operas become very accessible. These can readily be associated with contemporary Art Songs and Arias and help the inexperienced listener.

19. Comparing contemporary music with past developments and pointing out influences of the past can be very stimulating to classes made up of students who have had considerable listening experience.

20. Note the change from one period to another in the use of terms such as sonata, cantata, trio, symphony, concerto, etc.

21. Compare various composers' approach to the same subject such as Grofé's "Cloudburst" with the beginning of Wagner's Overture to *The Flying Dutchman;* Debussy's *Clouds* with Griffes' *Clouds;* Kodály's *Viennese Clock* with the slow movement of Haydn's "Clock" Symphony; etc.

22. Note how some periods tend to leave an influence on some particular composition or compositions of some composers, such as the Impressionistic influence on Grofé's "Sunrise"; the Classic form in Prokofiev's symphonies; the Romanticism in many early compositions of Samuel Barber; etc.

23. Compare program music and absolute music in all

166

periods. This is especially helpful in Impressionistic and Expressionistic music.

24. Compare Realism, Impressionism, and Expressionism by sight and sound. Excellent slides are available through many sources. Realism may be defined as the world we live in; Impressionism, the world we imagine; Expressionism, the dream world that exists subconsciously.

25. The operettas of Johann Strauss, such as *Die Fledermaus,* are interesting preparation to nineteenth-century operas of the Romanticists.

26. Some students may be interested in the reasons back of certain compositions. A composition may be a commissioned work for a certain function, an experiment, or an inspired work that the composer felt compelled to write, or for any number of reasons. In all cases, it is best to refer to the composers and not to what others may have written about their compositions. So often these other writings are incorrect or artificial.

27. Some students may be interested in social and economic influences on the development of music in its early support by the Church, then its support by wealthy families and nobility, later by public concerts, and the present-day support by private subsidy and by governments.

28. Biographies of composers are an important part of a broader understanding of music. These are omitted in this book because brief sketches about composers are unsatisfactory; sometimes, because of their brevity, they are misleading.

29. The Questionnaire in the back of the book not only helps the instructor become acquainted with the student but gives the student a better idea of his strong and weak areas of knowledge.

30. The work sheets are important in developing positive listening whether you come up with the right answer or not. In a class it is interesting to get an average of the scores.

Name _____

MY RECORD LIBRARY

_____

_____

_____

_____

_____

_____

_____

_____

_____

_____

_____

_____

_____

_____

_____

_____

_____

_____

_____

Name _____

MY RECORD LIBRARY

_____

_____

_____

_____

_____

_____

_____

_____

_____

_____

_____

_____

_____

_____

_____

_____

_____

_____

_____

Name_____ Section_____

WORK SHEET NO. 1

Check the instruments that you hear.

		1	2	3	4	5	6	7	8	9	10	11	12
STRING	Violin												
	Viola												
	Cello												
	Doublebass												
	Harp												
	Harpsichord												
	Piano												
WOODWIND	Piccolo												
	Flute												
	Clarinet												
	Saxophone												
	Oboe												
	English Horn												
	Bassoon												
BRASS	Trumpet												
	French Horn												
	Trombone												
	Tuba												
PERCUSSION	Kettledrum												
	Bass Drum												
	Snare Drum												
	Cymbals												
	Triangle												
	Xylophone												
	Celesta												
	Other												

WORK SHEET NO. 2

Andante con moto, Symphony No. 5, Beethoven

Check the choirs that play part or all of the following:		String Choir	Woodwind Choir	Brass Choir
I – Theme	1			
Echo passage	2			
II – 1st period – Theme	3			
II – 2nd period – Theme	4			
I – Variation No. 1	5			
II – 1st period – Variation No. 1	6			
II – 2nd period – Variation No. 1	7			
I – Variation No. 2	8			
I – Variation No. 3	9			
I – Variation No. 4	10			
Interlude	11			
II – 2nd period – Theme	12			
Returning passage – Retransition	13			
I – Theme	14			
Coda	15			

Name_____ Section_____

Name of band or orchestra _____

WORK SHEET NO. 3

Sketch in a seating plan of some particular band or orchestra. Do not copy conventional plan given in this book.

WORK SHEET NO. 4

Check any of these expressive qualities that you hear in the music	Composition	1	2	3	4	5	6
Amorous							
Brilliant							
Calm							
Charming							
Delicate							
Devotional							
Doleful							
Dramatic							
Festive							
Gay							
Gloomy							
Glorious							
Graceful							
Heroic							
Joyous							
Majestic							
Melancholy							
Mysterious							
Noisy							
Pleasant							
Sad							
Serious							
Singable							
Sinister							
Thrilling							
Turbulent							
Vigorous							
Other							

177

WORK SHEET NO. 5

Check the qualities or characteristics that you hear.

	1	2	3	4	5	6	7	8
RHYTHM								
Easy to follow								
Difficult to follow								
MELODY								
Clear, distinct								
Songlike								
Vague								
Unpredictable								
Obscure								
EMOTION								
Suppressed								
Restrained								
Unrestrained								
Emphasized								
TONE COLORS								
Colorless								
Transparent								
Colorful								
Atmospheric								
QUALITIES OF								
Renaissance								
Baroque								
Rococo								
Classic								
Romantic								
Impressionistic								
Expressionistic								
Neo-Classic								
Post-Romantic								
Popular								
MEDIUM OR FORM (Write in) (Examples: string quartet, vocal solo, organ solo, orchestra, piano concerto, etc.)								
	1	2	3	4	5	6	7	8

Questionnaire

Name_____ Section_____ Date_____
      (Please print last name first)

Home town and state _____

Year in school_____ Major_____

HOME ENVIRONMENT (Check only when the answer is "yes.")

    1. Are either of your parents interested in music? Enthusiastic?

    2. Does your home have TV?   Radio? Record player (LP)?

    3. Does your family have an LP "Classical" library? Jazz   Popular?

    4. Has your family attended any of the following? If more than once, double-check. Artist concert series?   Opera?   Symphony? Ballet?   Musical comedy?   Jazz concert?   String quartet concert?   Soloist (instrumental or vocal)?

YOUR LISTENING EXPERIENCE (Check only when answer is "yes.")

    1. Have you attended a concert by a major symphony orchestra?   Soloist?   String quartet Opera?   Operetta?   Band? Big name jazz band?   Musical comedy? An artist concert series?

    2. Do you arrange your work so that you may be able to attend concerts and musical events on the campus?

    3. How many concerts have you heard during the past year?

    4. Check the kind of music you like best (one or more). Symphony   Band   Opera Operetta   Ballet   Concertos Organ   Piano   Violin   Vocal solos   Vocal groups   String Quartet Jazz

Questionnaire (Cont.)

5. Have you a "classical" record collection?
   Popular?   Jazz?

6. Do you expect to start a "classical" record collection?   Jazz?   Popular?

7. Do you listen to recorded music with friends?
   Often?   Occasionally?

8. Do you discuss the music with your friends before playing?   During the playing?
   After?

9. Have you ever followed the score of any music while listening to it?

10. Do you own: A music dictionary?   A history of music?   Another book on music appreciation?   Biography of any composer?
    Any other book about music?

11. Have you read a book about music during the past year?   Name it.

12. Are you a subscriber to a music magazine?
    Name it.

YOUR PARTICIPATION EXPERIENCE (Check only when answer is "yes.")

1. Do you play a musical instrument?
   Name it.   Sing?

2. Have you played in a high school orchestra?
   Band?   Years experience?

3. Have you sung in a high school choral organization?   Years?

4. Are you playing or singing in the college orchestra?
   Band?   Organized vocal group?
   Church choir?

5. During the past year have you sung a solo?
   Played an instrumental solo?

INDEX

Anthem: Handel's *Zadok the Priest*, 45; Baroque composers of, 49
Art song: defined and discussed, 84; listening techniques, 84–86
—*The Erlking* (Schubert): discussed, 86–87
—suggested examples: Romantic, 87–88; Post-Romantic, 103

B

Bach, Carl Philipp Emanuel (1714–1788) (Pre-Classic): suggested compositions, 54, 55
Bach, Johann Christian (1735–1782) (Pre-Classic): suggested compositions, 54, 55, 139
Bach, Johann Sebastian (1685–1750) (Baroque): expressive qualities in, 32; use of timpani, 34; about suites, 35, 78; structure of concerto, 36; sonatas (various types) defined and discussed, 38–39; fugues discussed—analysis of exposition of G Major and g minor fugues, 40–41; cantatas defined and discussed, 46; scale temperament, 107
—suggested compositions: 23, 35, 36, 37, 39, 41, 43, 44, 46, 47, 48, 50
Balakirev, Mily (1837–1910) (Romantic): Russian "Five," 81; suggested composition, 82
Ballad: Italian ballad, 29
Ballet music: discussed, 77–78

—suggested examples: Rococo, 57; Romantic, 78–79; Twentieth-Century, 127–29
Band music. *See* Wind instruments, suggested music for
Barber, Samuel (1910–   ) (American): program and musical qualities of *Medea*, 113
—suggested compositions: 115, 122, 126, 127, 131, 132, 133, 141
Baroque Period (1600–1750): characteristics of, 32–33
—discussion of and suggested compositions: Baroque orchestra, 33–35; concerto, 35–37; concerto grosso, 37; sonata, 38–39; sonata chiesa, 38–39; sonata da camera, 38–39; trio sonata, 38–39; chamber music, 38–39; fugue, 39–41; organ music, 41–43; harpsichord music, 44; ceremonial music, 44–45; cantata, 46–47; oratorio, 47–48; motet, 48–49; opera, 49; miscellaneous vocal, 49–51
Bartók, Béla (1881–1945): suggested compositions, 119, 122, 123, 126, 131
Bassoon concerto: Mozart's, 23
Beethoven, Ludwig van (1770–1827) Classic): cello concerto, 55 used, 59; characteristics of early music, 59; analysis of Fifth Symphony, 60–64; "Pastorale" programmatic content, 64; characteristics of piano concertos, 65;

183

Children's music: helping your child, 143–45; choosing music, 144–45; appropriate program music, 145–46; on identifying instruments, 146; approach to the symphony, 147
—suggested music: symphonic poems and descriptive suites, 145–46; instruments of the orchestra, 146; symphonies, 147
Chopin, Frédéric (1810–1849) (Romantic): dissonance in compositions, 112
—suggested compositions: 78, 83
Choral. Suggested miscellaneous: Baroque, 49–51; Romantic, 89–91; Twentieth-Century, 133–36
Choral symphonies. *See* Symphonies, choral
Chorale Prelude: organ choral prelude defined and discussed, 41–42
—suggested examples: Baroque, 42, 43; Romantic, 84
Clarinet concerto: Mozart's, 140
Classic Period (1750–1825): organization of classic orchestra, 58–59; characteristics of instrumental music, 59; typical classic sonata, 60; typical symphony, 60; analysis of Beethoven's Fifth Symphony, 60–64; suggested Mozart, Haydn, and Beethoven symphonies, 64; concerti and suggested examples, 65–66; chamber music and suggested examples, 66–67; piano sonatas, 67–68; overtures, 68; Masses, 68–69
Color: an element, 4; psychological meaning in music, 4
Concerto: introduced by Torelli, 36; typical Baroque, 35–36; Classic, 65. *See also* Cello, Clarinet, Flute, Flute and harp, Guitar, Harp, Horn, Oboe, Organ, Piano, Trumpet, Violin, and guitar concerti and harpsichord, flute, and violin, 37; violin, cello, and piano, 66
—Harpsichord, suggested examples: Baroque, 36; Poulenc's, 123; three harpsichords, 37
—Piano, suggested examples: Classic, 65; Romantic, 83; Ravel's, 99; Rachmaninoff's, 103; Schönberg's,

111; other Twentieth-Century, 122–25 *passim;* two pianos: Mozart's, 66; Poulenc's, 124
—Violin, suggested examples: Baroque, 36; two violins, 36, 37; three violins, 37; Classic, 66; Romantic, 83; Expressionistic, 111; Sibelius', 103; Imbrie's, 123; Prokofiev's, 124
Concerto grosso: defined and discussed, 37; suggested examples, Baroque, 37, 139; Pre-Classic, 56
Copland, Aaron (1900–) (American): suggested compositions, 127, 129, 131
Corelli, Arcangelo (1653–1713) (Baroque): suggested compositions, 36, 37, 39
Couperin, François (1668–1733) (Pre-Classic): suggested compositions, 54, 55
Cui, César (1835–1918) (Romantic): Russian "Five," 81; *Orientale,* 82
Cycle, song. *See* Song cycle

D

Dahl, Ingolf (1912–): brass ensemble, 142
Debussy, Claude (1862–1918) (Impressionistic): main representative of Impressionism, 94; oriental influence, 94; compared with other Impressionists, 94; preference for whole-tone scale, 95; *Clouds,* 97; public acceptance of his music, 107, 112
—suggested compositions: 97, 98, 99
Delibes, Léo (1836–1891) (Romantic): place in history of ballet music, 78; suggested ballet music, 78
Delius, Frederick (1862–1934) (Impressionistic): Romantic tendencies, 94; compared with other Impressionists, 94; suggested compositions, 98
Divertimento: discussed, 53
—suggested examples: Haydn's, 56, 139; Mozart's, 56, 140; Bartók's, 131
Dohnányi, Ernst von (1877–1960): Variations for Piano and Orchestra, 125
Donizetti, Gaetano (1797–1848) (Romantic): Opera, 92

(Romantic): suggested compositions, 78, 83

Glinka, Michael (1804–1857) (Romantic): importance of *A Life for the Tsar*, 81
—suggested compositions, 77, 81

Gloria: Vivaldi's, 51

Gluck, Christoph Willibald (1714–1787) (Pre-Classic): suggested opera, 56; use of harp, 71; ideas about operatic overture, 77

Goldmark, Karl (1830–1915) (Romantic): symphony, 75; children's music, 147

Gould, Morton (1913–) (American): suggested compositions, 116, 120

Gounod, Charles (1818–1893) (Romantic): *Faust*, 92

Granados, Enrique (1867–1916) (Romantic): suggested composition illustrating Spanish nationalism, 81

Gregorian Chant: defined and discussed, 24–25

Grieg, Edvard (1843–1907) (Romantic): suggested compositions, 80, 81, 83, 145

Griffes, Charles Tomlinson (1884–1920) (American Impressionistic): style of Impressionism, 94; compared with other Impressionists, 94
—suggested composition, 98

Grofé, Ferde (1892–) (American): suggested suite, 120

Guitar: Rodrigo's Concerto for Guitar, 124

Guitars: Vivaldi's Concerto for Two Guitars, 36–37

H

Halle, Adam de la (*c.* 1240–1287) (Pre-Renaissance): secular music mentioned, 25

Handel, George Frideric (1685–1759) (Baroque): rhythm of "Hallelujah Chorus," 33; George II patronage, 45; use of harp, 71
—suggested compositions: 35, 36, 37, 44, 45, 48, 50, 139

Hanson, Howard (1896–) (American): illustrates orchestral tone color, 22
—suggested compositions: 22, 116, 141

Harmony: an element, 3; meaning of, to listener, 3–4

Harp concerto: Boieldieu's, 23

Harp serenade: Rodrigo's, 125

Harpsichord, Flute, and Violin Concerto: Bach's, 37

Harpsichord solos: *See* Suite. *See also* Sonata

Harris, Roy (1898–) (American): suggested compositions, 116, 141

Haydn, Franz Joseph (1732–1809) (Classic): early style of composing, 52, 53; influence on early orchestra, 58; instruments used by, 58; characteristics of music, 59; tonalities preceding time of, 106–7; mentioned in regard to dissonance, 112; "Clock" Symphony for children, 147
—suggested compositions of, 23, 53, 55, 56, 64, 66–69 *passim*, 139, 140

Hindemith, Paul (1895–1963): saxophone in orchestration, 72
—suggested compositions, 116, 120, 132, 141, 142

Holst, Gustav (1874–1934): suggested compositions, 120, 141

Honegger, Arthur (1892–1955): Oratorio, 134

Horn concerti: Mozart's, 140

I

Ibert, Jacques (1890–1962): suggested compositions, 120–21

Imbrie, Andrew (1914–) (American): violin concerto, 123

Impressionist Movement (1890–1925): characteristics of, 93–95; discussion of: influence of painters and poets, 93; technical phases, 95–96; listening techniques, 96–97
—suggested music: orchestral compositions, 97–98; piano music, 98; miscellaneous, 99

Incidental music: defined and discussed, 79
—suggested examples: Romantic, 79, 80; Twentieth-Century, 129–31

Instruments of the Orchestra: choirs, 5–6; families, 6; description of, 6; timbre, 6; orchestral tone color, 6; seating chart, 7; general comparisons, 19–21; identifying by timbre, 21–23; Renaissance, 30; Baroque orchestra, 33–35; Classic

Instruments *(continued)*
orchestra, 58–59; Romantic additions to the orchestra, 71–72. *See also* Orchestra

Ippolitov-Ivanov, Michael (1859–1935) (Romantic): "In the Village" example of exoticism in Russian music, 82

Isaac, Heinrich (*c.* 1450–1517) (Renaissance): suggested compositions, 29

Ives, Charles (1874–1954) (American): suggested compositions, 117, 121

J

Janácek, Leos (1854–1928): suggested compositions, 117, 134–35

Janequin, Clément (*c.* 1485–*c.* 1560) (Renaissance): chansons mentioned, 29

Jazz idioms: suggested examples: Gould, 120; Gershwin, 123; Milhaud, 128

Josquin des Prés (*c.* 1450–1521) (Renaissance): suggested Mass, 29

K

Khachaturian, Aram (1903–): suggested compositions, 82, 123, 128

Kodály, Zoltán (1882–): suggested compositions, 81, 121, 135, 145, 147

L

Lalande, Michel Richard de (1657–1726) (Baroque): suggested compositions, 45, 50

Lalo, Édouard (1823–1892) (Romantic): suggested composition, 83

Lambert, Constant (1905–1951): ballet music, 78
—suggested music, 79

Lassus, Orlandus (1532–1594) (Renaissance): suggested motets and Masses, 29

Le Jeune, Claude (1528–1600) (Renaissance): chansons mentioned, 29

Leoncavallo, Ruggiero (1858–1919) (Romantic): opera, 92

Liadov, Anatol (1855–1914) (Romantic): music for children, 145

Lieder. See Art Song

Listening aids and techniques: elements, 3–4; descriptions of instruments, 6–21; identifying timbre of instruments, 21–23; polyphonic music, 30–31; listening to fugues, 41; sonata-allegro form, an aid to listening, 60–61; choosing chamber music, 66, 82; symphonic poems, 72–73, 102; enjoying incidental music, 79; art songs, 84–86; song cycles, 88; long choral works, 98; opera, 91–92; Impressionism, 96–97; Mahler's *Resurrection*, 101; Expressionism, 109–10; Schuman Symphony No. 8, contemporary, 118; "experimental" listening, 137

Liszt, Franz (1811–1886) (Romantic): use of harp in orchestra, 71; presented first symphonic poem, 72; ideas of freedom, 72; *Les Preludes* discussed and analyzed, 73–74
—suggested compositions: 75, 83, 84, 87

Luening, Otto (1900–) (American): electronic music, 136

Lully, Jean-Baptiste (1632–1687) (Baroque): suggested compositions, 45, 46

M

MacDowell, Edward (1861–1908) (American Romantic): first recognized in Europe, 114; piano concerto, 83

Machaut, Guillaume de (*c.* 1300–1377) (Pre-Renaissance): first Mass composed throughout by one composer, 25; *La Messe de Nostre Dame,* 25

Madrigal: beginning of, 24; Renaissance, defined and discussed, 26–27; Italian madrigals, 29; English madrigals, 29
—suggested examples: Monteverdi's, 50

Magnificat: Scheidt's, 51

Mahler, Gustav (1860–1911) (Post-Romantic): *Resurrection* symphony discussed, 101; *Das Lied von der Erde* discussed, 101; about performance of one of his symphonies, 109

Toccata *(continued)*
—suggested toccatas: Baroque, 41, 43; Chávez' (percussion), 131
Torelli, Giuseppe (1658–1709) (Baroque): first to compose concerto, 36
—suggested compositions, 36, 37, 139
Trio: on selecting, 66
—suggested piano trios: Classic, 67; Romantic, 82, 83
—suggested string trios: Classic, 67. *See also* Sonata
Trumpet concerti: Torelli's, 139; Haydn's, 140; two trumpets, Manfredini's, 139; three trumpets, Telemann's, 140
Twentieth-Century music: characteristics of, 112–15; American music, 114–15; Neo-Classicism, 114
—suggested examples, instrumental symphonies: 115–19; orchestral suites, 119–22; concerti, 122–25; miscellaneous solo instruments and orchestra, 125–26; small ensembles, 126–27; ballet, 127–29; miscellaneous instrumental, 131–32
—suggested examples, vocal: operas, 132–33; miscellaneous, 133–36
—electronic: 136–37

U

Ussachevsky, Vladimir (1911–   ): Electronic music, 136

V

Varèse, Edgar (1885–1965): "Ionisation," 127; electronic music, 136; his ideas about the listener, 137
Variations: defined and discussed, 62; Corelli's *La Follia*, 39; in Andante Con Moto of Beethoven's Fifth Symphony, 62; Dohnányi's, 125
Vaughan Williams, Ralph (1872–1958): pipe organ in symphony, 72
—suggested compositions: 119, 130, 141
Verdi, Giuseppe (1813–1901 (Romantic): *Requiem*, 91; operas, 92
Victoria, Thomás Luis de (*c.* 1548–1611) (Renaissance): *Requiem*, 29
Vieuxtemps, Henri (1820–1881) (Ro-

mantic): violin concerto, 83
Villa-Lobos, Heitor (1887–1959): suggested compositions, 131, 135
Violin concerto. *See* Concerto
Violin sonata. *See* Sonata
Vittoria, Thomás Luis de. *See* Victoria (same as)
Vivaldi, Antonio (*c.* 1675–1741) (Baroque): place in early program music, 72
—suggested compositions: 23, 36, 37, 51

W

Wagner, Richard (1813–1883) (Romantic): use of harp in orchestral music, 71
—suggested compositions, 77, 88, 92
Walther, Johann Gottfried (1684–1748) (Baroque): suggested organ music, 44
Weber, Carl Maria von (1786–1826) (Romantic): suggested compositions, 77, 80
Webern, Anton (1883–1945) (Expressionistic): a leading figure in Expressionistic movement, 105
—suggested compositions, 110
Widor, Charles Marie (1845–1937) (Romantic): suggested organ music, 84
Wieniawski, Henri (1835–1880) (Romantic): suggested violin concerto, 83
Wind instruments: suggested music for:
—Renaissance: brass and pipe organ, 139
—Baroque: chamber music, 139; concerti, 23, 139; suite, 139; concerto grosso, 139
—Pre-Classic: chamber music, 139–40; concerto for three trumpets, 140
—Classic: chamber music, 140; concerti, 140; marches, 140; serenades, 141
—Romantic: Schumann's *Konzertstück* for Four Horns and Orchestra, 141
—Twentieth-Century: band, 141; chamber music, 142; large brass choir and string orchestra, 142
Wolf, Hugo (1860–1903) (Romantic): importance of composer in the art songs, 84; suggested art song and song cycle, 88